The Decorated Tile

An Illustrated History of English Tile-making and Design

J & B AUSTWICK

CHARLES SCRIBNER'S SONS
NEW YORK

First U.S. edition published by Charles
Scribner's Sons 1981

ISBN: 0 684 16761 1

Library of Congress Catalog Number
80–52107

Text set in 11/13 pt. Baskerville
by Granada Graphics
and printed in Great Britain by
W S Cowell Ltd Ipswich

Designed by Fred Price

Previous page: Illustrations show detail from
Campbell Tile Co. catalogues. 1a (above) is
c 1890, 1b is *c* 1882.

Contents

Acknowledgements

A successful conclusion to a work of this kind can only be achieved with the involvement and assistance of a large number of people, and we would like to take this opportunity of expressing our thanks to all those who have helped either with information or by providing facilities in which to conduct our research. Firstly, Matthew Townsend, who at his shop in Alfies Antique Market, London, has allowed us to study his boundless and constantly changing stock of tiles. The same is true of the other specialist dealers, Paddy Frost (Delft and Victorian tiles) and Kathy Brunner (Art Nouveau), both of Antiquarius Ltd., Chelsea, who have always shown us the greatest courtesy on our frequent visits. Others to whom we owe a debt of gratitude for their invaluable help are Robert Copeland, historical adviser to Spode Ltd.; Paul Atterbury, historical adviser to Royal Doulton Tableware Ltd.; Tony Herbert and his staff at the Ironbridge Gorge Museums; Dr. Celoria of the Gladstone Pottery Museum; Gaye Blake Roberts of the Wedgwood Museum; Pat Halfpenny of the City Museum and Art Gallery, Stoke-on-Trent; Dr. Fraser at Keele University; Mr. Tom Harrison of Pilkingtons Tiles Ltd. (Poole); Mary McLoughlin of Pilkingtons Tiles Ltd. (Manchester); Carol Baron of Close Antiques, Winchester; the Warden and Fellows of Winchester College; Mr. David Malkin, historical adviser to H. & R. Johnson Ltd.; George Wooliscroft & Sons Ltd.; and Eric Knowles of Bonhams. We would also like to thank the following museums, libraries and institutions for their help and advice in searching out often very elusive information: the Victoria and Albert Museum; The British Library, particularly the staff of the Keen Street Annex; the reference libraries of Hanley, Hereford, Winchester, Derby, Shrewsbury, Swinton and Fareham; the Royal Photographic Society; The Royal Institute of British Architects; the Public Record Office, Kew; and Sotheby's, Belgravia.

Finally, we would like to thank that devoted band of collectors, and Mr. J. S. M. Scott in particular, who have allowed us to photograph their private collections. To these and everyone we have met during our travels we offer a heartfelt thank you and hope that this book meets with their approval, and lives up to their expectations.

Photographic Acknowledgements

All photographs are by Brian Austwick, AIIP, for Jack and Jill Tiles, Antique Market, Winchester, except for those indicated below by an asterisk.

The authors and publisher would like to thank the following individuals and organizations for permitting either their tiles to be photographed or their photographs to be reproduced. (The numbers are illustration numbers.)

The British Library: 93, 96-98, 160, 233.

*The British Museum: 7.

City Museum and Art Gallery, Stoke-on-Trent: 27, 28, 30, 67, 231, 301.

Gladstone Pottery Museum: 31, 61, 62, 99, 102, 140, 228, 229, 235, 250, 282.

Horace Barks Reference Library, Stoke-on-Trent (Staffordshire County Council): 32.

*Angelo Hornak/Vision International: 339.

Ironbridge Gorge Museum: 2, 63, 100, 156, 158, 196, 278, 325.

*Lucinda Lambton Library: 88, 89, 91, 92, 94, 95, 223, 276, 309, 343.

*Michelin Tyre Co. Ltd.: 326, 327.

Pilkingtons Tiles Ltd.: 192, 193, 203, 204, 206, *344-6.

*Ronald Sheridan: 9, 10, 13.

Royal Doulton Tableware Ltd.: 49, 106 (also on jacket front, right), 108, 121, 125-7, 262-75, 290, 291, 295, 321.

Spode Ltd.: 141-6, 150, 151, 154.

*Sussex Archaeological Society: 8.

*Victoria and Albert Museum/Michael Holford Library: 11.

Warden and Fellows of Winchester College: 14 (also on jacket front, bottom left), 15, 16, *17 (photograph by E. A. Sollars).

Wedgwood Museum Trustees, Barlaston: 188, 248.

*Woodmansterne Publications Ltd.: 12 (photograph by Howard C. Moore).

Introduction

Since the potters of the ancient world discovered the fine art of decorating the thin slabs of clay that we now call tiles, their use has become so widespread and their applications so varied, that there is a danger of taking them for granted, and yet the reasons for their universal acceptance have changed little since the ancient Egyptians and the Babylonians erected their monuments to the glory of their kings and deities. It is a fitting tribute to the tile makers' skill and the tile's durability, that many of the tiles or, more properly, enamelled bricks from these legendary buildings have survived. As a means of decoration the tile is unsurpassable for quality and purity of colour, which when dimmed by accumulated layers of grime, needs little more than a shower of rain or the wipe of a cloth to restore its original lustrous condition. The design and method of decoration on the earliest tiles were subject to the many diverse cultural backgrounds within their country of origin, but as trade routes opened up, the various design influences spread throughout the world. In later years, our Victorian forefathers were to draw heavily on the designs and motifs from the ancient world, adapting them where necessary to suit the acceptable standards of contemporary good taste.

Improving social and economic conditions brought about by a marked advancement in industrial technology stimulated demand for new and improved buildings. It was this atmosphere which fostered the Gothic revival, begun in 1817, with its return to medieval architecture and form, under the advocacy of its leading exponent, architect Augustus Pugin. While he could design the buildings readily enough, the practical architectural detail was more problematic. For more than three hundred years the art of making medieval floor tiles had been lost, and though modern, plain quarry tiles were available to Pugin, he sought faithful reproductions of the old tiles.

Pugin worked with Herbert Minton in an effort to re-create the medieval floors, and after a great deal of trial and error, Minton finally succeeded in his endeavours. He adapted the techniques for industrial production, and was highly successful in adopting Richard Prosser's method of dust pressing tiles. Until then tiles had been made by hand in "plastic" clay, but dust pressing was a timely mechanical means of meeting the increasing demand for the new tiles. Before long, every building which laid a claim to being fashionable had tiled floors and pavements. New tile manufacturers sprang up all over the country. Every major exhibition throughout the world had a large contingent from the British tile industry, which was usually successful in taking the lion's share of the awards. As sanitary conditions improved, a need for wall tiles was created, and new methods were found to meet the demand for a lighter tile suitable for wall fixing. The wall tiles lent themselves to many different forms of decoration which would have been impractical if used on the floor, and impressed and embossed tiles became popular. Various methods of printing were tried and different techniques abounded. Very soon, every respectable building was able to complement its tiled floors with tiled dados, cloakrooms, fireplaces, ceilings — the list of potential uses was endless. Tiles were used to decorate hospitals, underground railway stations and ships because they were impervious to water, and were easy to clean and keep sterile.

Because of the vast quantity of tiles that was being produced, and the subsequent cheapening of the product, even the poorest families were able to afford them. Eventually the fashion for tiles

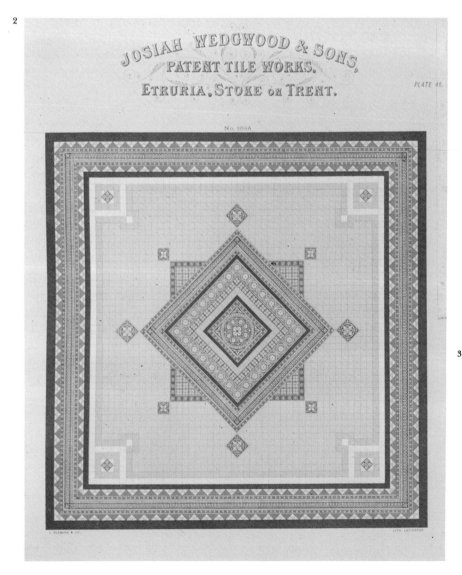

2. A page from the Wedgwood catalogue *c* 1885.
3. "March" from the popular *Old English* Wedgwood series *c* 1878.

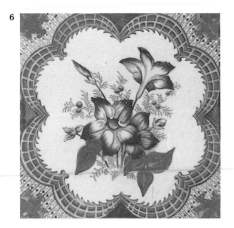

4-6. Typical transfer-printed and hand-coloured floral tiles of the 1880s and '90s. 4 was produced by at least five different companies.

became an obsession. Tiles were everywhere: in the bathroom, the bedroom, the kitchen, even in the garden; if they were not fixed to the walls or floors, they were incorporated into the furniture.

A rebellion was imminent and it came in the 1860s and '70s in the guise of the Arts and Crafts Movement, whose ideals were to turn away from industrial mass production and return to more individualized methods in both design and technique.

Influential designers of the day, Burne-Jones, William Morris, De Morgan, and Walter Crane put new life back into tile design, and brought quality back to the industry. Their designs were extremely popular and before long manufacturers were imitating and mass producing them. The public responded, but tiles were used only where appropriate, not to adorn every surface in sight.

The tile industry began a gradual decline, and though it enjoyed renewed activity when Art Nouveau and Art Deco were at their height, businesses closed down. By the 1930s tiles were considered old-fashioned. They were too heavy and too big for the more compact living accommodation, and though some companies still prospered, others closed down or concentrated their efforts on making tiles in plain or mottled glazes. The advent of World War II sealed the fate of the tile industry. In post-war rebuilding tiles had only a minor part to play in the new decorative schemes.

The opening up of new export markets in the 1950s offered the ailing industry a glimmer of hope. To counteract the effect of import duties levied on the weight of imported tiles, the manufacturers started to produce greater quantities of thinner, lighter tiles, which meant that lighter adhesives could be used, bringing the average tiling job within the scope of the home handyman. The decorated tile started to make a comeback, but the industry never again reached the dizzy heights of creative fashionability of the 1880s and '90s.

With the wholesale demolition of much of Victorian Britain during the last two decades, many millions of tiles have been destroyed and it is only recently that an interest in this neglected field of Victorian endeavour has been rekindled. The demand for Victorian tiles now far outstrips the supply. They are much sought after by collectors. Interior designers make widespread use of the old tiles both in modern settings or in the restoration of Victorian and Edwardian properties. The serious students of design seek inspiration in the styles and methods used on the tiles in just the same way as their predecessors sought inspiration from the past.

Surprisingly there are only a few museums in England that have decorated tiles permanently on display. Among them are the Victoria and Albert Museum, London; the Gladstone Pottery Museum, Longton, Staffordshire; and the City Museum, Stoke-on-Trent, whose tile display opens at the end of 1980. The Ironbridge Gorge Museum, Telford, Shropshire, is planning to open a major permanent tile exhibition by 1982.

Tiles amply repay the time and effort spent in seeking them out. Whether one buys them from a dealer, rescues them from a demolition site or views them in a museum, they provide a fascinating insight into a way of life long gone but far from forgotten.

9

CHAPTER ONE

The Early History of the Tile

The development of the decorated tile is not an easy one to trace in a chronological sequence since many different civilizations were perfecting their own techniques independently, but among the earliest examples known are the glazed bricks and tiles of ancient Egypt, some of which date back to the fourth millenium B.C. From these developed finely inlaid and incised tiles filled in counter relief and usually finished in transparent, turquoise-blue glazes, the subjects ranging from the native flora and fauna to scenes of conquest and slavery. Decorated tilework was reserved for the upper eschelons of society; most people could only look and admire from a distance. At about the same time, the Cretans were engaged in developing architectural ceramics and their faience plaques, mosaics and modelled reliefs display a much higher standard of competence than their Egyptian counterparts.

Further East, King Nebuchadnezzar (604-562 B.C.) erected the celebrated Tower of Babel in Babylon, to the glory of the seven planets, each of which was represented by successive storeys

7

7. Early floor mosaic from Harlicarnassus in Turkey.

8. 2nd-century "Medusa" mosaic floor overlying 1st-century geometric mosaic at the Roman palace, Fishbourne, Sussex.

constructed of appropriately coloured glazed bricks. In another part of the city was a series of enamelled brick reliefs depicting lions, dragons, bulls and other mythical and sacred creatures, which are some of the first examples of tiles and bricks being prepared individually and assembled on site to create the finished mural. Geometric and other designs are also known to have been constructed using the same methods. Excavations at Nimrud have revealed that in 845 B.C. the neighbouring Assyrians, whose culture was closely linked to that of Babylonia, constructed the same characteristic relief wall panels in conjunction with architectural terracotta which incorporated a string course of decorated tilework.

With the opening of trade routes, the art of tile making gradually spread across the East, through Persia, Syria and Turkey, and on to India where it met with influences travelling westward from China and Mongolia. The first true wall tiles originated from Persia and legend relates that the lustre tiles used at Sidi Okba were made by a craftsman from Baghdad in A.D. 894. By the thirteenth century the Persian decorated tile industry was flourishing. Two hundred years later the character of the decoration had changed from star shaped and rectangular relief tiles to the pronounced foliated ornament, usually in blue and green, which reflected the same patterns of leaves, flowers and birds as the magnificent carpets of the region. As the Chinese influence reached Persia the characteristic blue-on-white decoration, which was to become so popular

11

in Europe, became fashionable and in due course was copied by the Syrians whose tile industry was centred around Damascus.

As the nomadic Mohammedan Arabs, the Saracens, roamed throughout the Middle East, conquering Syria, Persia, Mesopotamia, Egypt and Numidia, their respective cultures became interlinked and spread throughout the whole of Moorish North Africa and up into Spain, where they met and fused with Christian heraldry. Throughout all these lands was an underlying influence from the Roman Empire, particularly in the east where the Byzantine architectural influence had spread as far as Russia, carrying with it the traditional Roman skills of mosaic in glass, marble and ceramic.

Meanwhile, in northern Europe inlaid tiles, which were admirably suited for use on the floor, were rapidly gaining in popularity as a welcome relief to the drabness of flagstones. The use of tiles on the floor was peculiar to Europe at this time; by tradition the Arabic and Asiatic countries had always covered their floors with brightly coloured carpets which complemented their wall tiling, but the Europeans favoured a more austere approach to the decoration of their cathedrals and palaces.

The exact date of the introduction of floor tiles to England will always be open to speculation. Certainly, well before the thirteenth century, tiles from France and Spain were finding their way into the country; the first tiles to be made in England were the tile mosaics used by the monastic orders in the first part of the thirteenth century to pave their abbeys and cathedrals.

9. The Friday Mosque. Isfahan, Iran.
10. St. James Armenian Cathedral, Jerusalem. 11th century.
11. Persian lustre wall-tile from a mosque at Khonsar, Kashan. 14th century.

12. Confessor handing ring to pilgrim. Westminster Abbey *c* 1250.

The earliest pavements were built up of shaped components of alternate colours, which usually formed a simple geometric pattern, though there are examples of more complex shapes such as the fleur-de-lis and other Gothic motifs.

Inlaid tiles probably evolved from two independent sources. Firstly, by about 1250, the individual tiles in the mosaics began to be decorated by pressing a shaped wooden block into the surface of the unfired tile to create a counter relief or line pattern. The tile was otherwise left plain. It was only a matter of time before the indent was filled with a contrasting "slip" of white clay to produce the inlaid tile. After coating with a clear lead glaze, and subsequent firing, the tile appeared as a yellow pattern in a brown body. The second path which led to the evolution of the inlaid tile was the method employed to decorate stone flooring. The majority of floors at this time were paved with stone which could be decorated if the importance of the building was such that it warranted the extra expense and labour. A design was first of all drawn on the stone slab, after which the surrounding area was cut away to leave a shallow relief decoration. The sunken areas were then filled with a darker resinous substance so that the original design stood out light against a dark background. This was an extremely laborious process, not particularly hard wearing, and one which could be easily reproduced by impressing a design on a clay tablet and filling it in with a lighter coloured slip — in other words, the inlaid tile.

By the end of the thirteenth century, the irregular inlaid tile mosaics were rendered obsolete by the much cheaper, mass-produced square tiles. These tiles, which were 5 or 6 in (13 or 15 cm) square, were introduced around 1250 and rapidly gained popularity under the patronage of Henry III who used the new inlaid tiles in large numbers to pave the royal buildings. The Church was not slow to follow, and many cathedrals were paved with these tiles including Salisbury and Winchester. Winchester Cathedral has over five thousand decorated tiles surviving on its floor, with about sixty different patterns. The tiles were made by itinerant craftsmen who travelled to the sites of new buildings and set up their workshops there. Hence medieval tile kilns are found on a great many sites near cathedrals and royal palaces. Because the craftsmen used the same wooden dies at each site a large number of identical designs have been found at different locations. The flourishing medieval tile industry operated on a regional basis and each different "school" evolved its own characteristic style and technique. The most prominent in the thirteenth century was the Wessex School which encompassed the tile makers of Hampshire, Wiltshire, Dorset and Somerset, but by the later middle ages the industry was dominated by the tile manufacturers of London, the Midlands and the Chilterns.

The Chiltern tilers were the most commercially minded of all the medieval tile makers. By the middle of the fourteenth century they had perfected a method of printing a design onto a tile by dipping the wooden die into the white slip and applying it to the tile. This method reduced the amount of slip needed and minimized the labour content. They went further, and reduced the size of the tile

13. "Combat". Chertsey Abbey. 13th century.

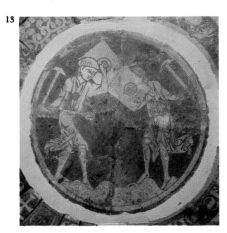

to about 4½ in (11 cm) square, which meant that they could reduce the thickness of the tile from the standard 1 in (2.5 cm), to ¾ in (2 cm) without the risk of warping in the kiln. The resulting tile was far cheaper than anyone else's and its popularity spread far beyond the normal regional boundaries. These tiles, however, were more prone to wear than the normal inlaid type and other areas, notably London, adapted a technique which was a compromise between the old technique and the new, whereby the design was pressed to just below the surface of the tile, making it less susceptible to wear. This type of tile dates from around the latter part of the fourteenth century. At about the same time, a thriving industry was building up in East Anglia, centred on Bawsey, near Kings Lynn, where the workshops produced relief tiles in green, brown and yellow glazes, decorated with the heraldic devices and fantastic creatures.

Variations on the basic designs and techniques proliferated throughout the regions. The most popular designs included geometric patterns made up from four or more tiles which were often decorated with fleur-de-lis, rosettes or armorial and heraldic devices. Single tiles very often depicted birds, lions, fantastic beasts, horsemen, heraldic devices, and the ubiquitous fleur-de-lis. Other rarer tiled schemes comprised whole tile pictures. The roundels from Chertsey Abbey are probably the best examples of this, where over thirty pictures illustrate the story of Tristram and Isolt, and nine others depict incidents from the life of Richard Coeur de Lion.

14-16. Wessex School. Inlaid Floor tiles
c 1300, 5 in × 5 in (13 cm × 13 cm).

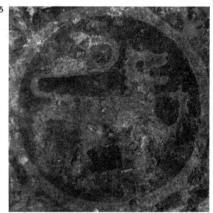

14

17. 14th-century floor tiles from Winchester College, Hampshire.

After the Reformation very few decorated tiles were made as there was a plentiful supply in the ruined abbeys and monasteries. Some tile makers managed to survive though, and inlaid tiles were being made long enough for Renaissance designs to be used on them. During the sixteenth century the old techniques were revived from time to time, but without any great enthusiasm since wooden flooring was far more comfortable, and if tiles were necessary, plain quarry tiles would suffice.

Slowly, however, as a result of an increasing awareness of the visual arts and a general move towards more comfortable homes brought about by the Renaissance, tin-glazed tiles with their bright colours and rich glazes were introduced by travellers who had been impressed by Continental tilework, and had brought tiles back with them to furnish their own apartments.

As trade relations between the Italians and the Moors improved after the crusades, a thriving industry in opaque glazed, or majolica, wares grew up around Urbino and Faenza towards the end of the fourteenth century, based on original Moorish techniques. From their workshops in Tuscany, Luca Della Robbia and his family created many fine tiled pavements in addition to some splendid devotional panels and tabernacles that were used in churches throughout the country. As the majolica tiles became

15

popular more workshops were set up and more tiled pavements
were laid embellished with typical Renaissance motifs: portraits in
profile, symbolic and heraldic devices, and animals and birds.
Despite the unquestionable skill of the decorators, the quality of
the tile bodies was poor and after a period of three hundred years
the manufacture of majolica had virtually ceased.

In Germany a tradition for relief tiles decorated with Gothic
tracery and other motifs in subdued green and brown glazes was
well established by the fourteenth century. These tiles were
principally used in and around stoves and their use was common
throughout neighbouring Austria and Switzerland. With the
arrival in Germany of itinerant Italian potters who brought with
them their majolica glazing techniques tin-glazed ware became
popular but tended to be very subdued in colour, sometimes almost
black, and completely lacking the sparkling qualities of the
authentic Italian majolica.

As the use of tin glazes spread, other important centres of tile
manufacture were established in France, Belgium — Antwerp in
particular — and Holland. From its beginnings at Lyons, French
tile manufacture quickly spread to Nevers, Rouen and Lille and in
a relatively short space of time, French tiles incorporated Italian,
Persian and Dutch influences. One of the greatest French potters
during the sixteenth century was Bernard Palissy who turned his
hand to practically every aspect of ceramics. His tiles are
characterized by the use of bright yellows, blues, greens and
browns, depicting figures and ornamental subjects.

The colourful faience from sixteenth-century Antwerp was
again heavily influenced by the Italian schools of Faenza and
Urbino. The most striking feature of these tiles is the use of vivid
yellow. In common with the rest of Europe, the tiles made there
were destined for use on the floor, but it was not long before they
made the transition to the walls where they were used to create
magnificent house signs and panels very often adapted from
contemporary engravings. As a result of the religious troubles that
beset Belgium at this time — Antwerp suffered a massacre of some
six thousand at the hands of the Spanish garrison stationed there
— the tile industry came to an abrupt halt and many potters moved
north to Holland.

18

19

18-19. 17th-century Dutch Delft tiles,
5 in × 5 in (13 cm × 13 cm).

Delft Tiles

The Dutch tile industry began its trade in the opening years of the
sixteenth century, a trade which was to mark a new era for the
decorated tile and which infiltrated into every country in Europe,
and a great many overseas, including North and South America;
though it was in Germany and Denmark that Dutch tiles found
their widest markets, and it was there that they were most widely
imitated.

The town of Delft which gave its name to the tin-glazed
earthenware that was made there ceased to be the most important

16

20-21. 18th-century Dutch Delft tiles,
5 in × 5 in (13 cm × 13 cm).

22. Bristol *c* 1770. Showing the
distinctive Bianco-Sopra-Bianco
borders.

centre of manufacture by about 1650. It was overtaken by the workshops of Rotterdam, Harlingen, Makkum, Utrecht and Haarlem. The early Dutch tiles were extremely colourful and much influenced by the Spanish reliance on geometric form. Soon tiring of the restraints this imposed, the Netherlands turned to Chinese methods of decoration in blue and white from which evolved the characteristic styles of traditional Dutch Delftware, with its use of freely painted scenes of everyday Dutch life. Corner devices were commonly added to give a sense of unity to the whole tiled arrangement when in position on a wall, and whole rooms were often covered from floor to ceiling with grandiose tiled schemes.

In every craft there are those who feel a need to move on and ply their trade in a new environment and the Dutch and Flemish potters were no exception. Just as their tiles were exported the world over, they too began to travel — some of them to England.

As early as 1520 a tiled floor decorated with fashionable Renaissance portraits and motifs was laid in the Chapel of The Vyne in Hampshire, using majolica tiles from Antwerp. Henry VIII used Flemish tiles to pave the floors at Hampton Court. Encouraged by these early successes, several of the potters from Antwerp settled in this country in the latter half of the sixteenth century, notably Jasper Andries who established a tile works in Norwich around 1567. Shortly afterwards, his partner Jacob Jansen moved to London where he produced tin-glazed paving tiles. Few tiles were made after Jansen's death, and those that were still remained for use on the floor in spite of an increasing Continental influence to apply them to the wall.

Decorated Dutch wall tiles were probably introduced to England in about 1630, again by returning travellers. By 1650 a few Dutch potters had come across from Holland to settle in and around London, bringing with them their traditional styles and techniques. It took until the turn of the century before they successfully adapted their techniques to working with English materials. To meet the demand which these potters had created, and had difficulty in supplying, tiles were exported from Holland in ever increasing numbers despite a ban on pottery imports.

When William of Orange acceded to the throne in 1689 the influence of Dutch culture began to pervade everything from furniture to fashion and, of course, tiles. William and Queen Mary decorated several rooms at Hampton Court with Dutch tiles (though he did not see fit to lift the ban on Dutch imports), and to a large degree set the tone of things to come. Five years before William came to the throne, the Delft potters were already establishing themselves in Bristol, where they commenced the manufacture of tin-glazed earthenware. English Delft tiles were not produced in any great quantity until after about 1730, by which time the potters had overcome all the initial production problems. Even by this time, the English tile was not as well thought of as its Dutch counterpart. The relatively soft sandy body of Dutch tiles (sometimes called "Sandy Backs") could easily be ground to fit into awkward places, whereas English tiles were hard and could only be

17

23

24

23. Bristol *c* 1750. With flower-head corners.
24. Bristol *c* 1720. A common subject on plates, unusual on tiles. Barred ox-head corners.

shaped with difficulty. At about this time some of the more successful potters from London moved to Liverpool and soon made that city the most important tile making centre in the country. Many of the old traditions were dispensed with, and while there was still a constant supply of the Dutch influenced designs painted in blue and manganese, new borders and patterns were introduced, and the colour palette was widened. Polychrome tiles decorated in reds, blues, yellows and greens became popular.

It can be extremely difficult to differentiate between early English Delft tiles and those of their Dutch rivals, but from about 1740 a characteristic English style began to emerge. The London tilers nearly always followed original Dutch designs, but Bristol became known for its wavy, white Bianco-Sopra-Bianco borders and its distinctive rococo landscapes, and Liverpool for its polychrome decorations and chinoiserie subjects. With the interchange of patterns and ideas between the two countries and the workshops within them, inevitable confusions occur when trying to attribute a tile to a particular area, but it is possible to make some generalizations about the different characteristics of English and Dutch Delft tiles. Probably the most important distinguishing feature is the glaze. On a Dutch tile, particularly those of the eighteenth century, the glaze is very white when compared to that on an English tile, which generally displays a faint blue or green

18

tint. The Dutch glaze is considerably less smooth than its English counterpart and is often very thin and dry in appearance. The English glaze tends to be rich and soft and feels very smooth to the touch. Later Liverpool tiles display an extremely high gloss.

The other major difference lies in the actual execution and style of the designs, many of which were based on contemporary engravings and prints of both countries. The usual Dutch method of applying the design was by means of a pricked stencil through which the design was pounced in charcoal onto the glazed but unfired surface of the tile biscuit. The artist literally had to join the dots and add any shading or fine detail that was required. Some Dutch tiles display extreme neatness when done by this method

25. Liverpool *c* 1760. Birds contained within a barbed medallion border.

25

but the poorer examples, probably painted by apprentices, show an appreciable lack of artistic imagination and are decorated with almost mechanical precision. The English tile makers managed to achieve a rather more spontaneous approach to the painting, while still retaining interest in the detail.

Corner patterns and borders on English tiles were usually based on Dutch originals, but very rarely were they exact copies. An excellent example of this adaption is the Dutch "ox head" border motif which evolved into the "barred ox-head" corner. Others were purely of English origin: the Liverpool potters designed a wide variety of original corner motifs and border patterns. The majority of these border patterns enhanced the tile scheme, but others exhibited lack of understanding on the designer's part as to the overall effect of the tiles when displayed together on a wall or fireplace. Though a tile might look most attractive by itself, the whole effect could be ruined if the sheer weight of the combined border patterns reduced the actual pattern on the tile to a position of insignificance.

19

Printed Tiles

One of the most significant events for the pottery industry was the introduction of transfer printing in the late 1740s. The early history of the technique is somewhat obscure, but two men laid claim independently to being the inventor of the process: John Brooks a printer from London, and John Sadler a printer from Liverpool. John Sadler was the first successfully to apply the technique to the mass production of tiles. In an affidavit sworn in July 1756, he and his associate, Guy Green, claimed to have printed twelve hundred tiles with differing patterns within the space of six hours: a volume of production that would previously have taken a hundred workmen, all producing the same design, to achieve. The process involved printing from a wood-block (later, an engraved copper plate) onto a prepared transfer paper, and applying it, printed-side-down to the glazed surface of the tile. After ensuring a good contact had been made the paper was floated off, leaving behind the print in ceramic colour. The tile was afterwards fired. Most of the designs were based on contemporary engravings and printed black and later coloured with enamels, though some were printed in either purple, blue or a rich brown colour.

The first tiles Sadler produced were wood-block prints and though technically successful, were not instantly popular. After a few months he changed to the newly introduced technique of

26

27

26. Rare tile by J. Sadler. Printed from a wood-block and decorated in overglaze enamels *c* 1756.
27. Rare Wedgwood tile printed from an engraving by T. Baddeley *c* 1800.

28

30

29

28. Rare Wedgwood tile. Copper-plate
engraved by T. Fletcher *c* 1795.
29. "The Ape and the Fox" *c* 1770.
Copper-plate print by Sadler & Green.
One of a series of Aesop's fables.
30. Original print from Fig. 28
published in *Temple of Taste* 1795.

transfer printing from copper plates. With an eye on the upper-class market he commissioned several engravers. The business expanded, he took Guy Green into partnership and at about the same time began experiments in decorating creamware for Josiah Wedgwood. By 1764 they were suitably organized and equipped to begin large-scale decoration of Wedgwood's creamware, at the expense of lost production of their own tiles. When Sadler retired in 1770, Green continued to print tiles for a further twelve years until his most important customer, Wedgwood, obtained his own facilities for printing creamware tiles and wares. Other small concerns began printing tiles: Richard Abbey, an apprentice at Sadler & Green, set himself up as a printer making tiles to order; and Thomas Fletcher and Thomas Baddeley of Hanley, Staffordshire, produced printed tiles on creamware blanks. After 1790 very little Delftware was produced in England. Dutch tiles continued to be imported for fireplaces as the English creamware tiles crazed far more when exposed to heat.

Tile making in England had now reached an impasse. There were to be no major new technological advances for nearly forty years. Attempts to re-create the medieval inlaid tiles were made sporadically, but it was not until the Gothic revival of Victorian times that a concentrated effort was made to rediscover the lost craft.

Until the nineteenth century, English tiles had always been a luxury that only the wealthy could afford. It was not until Herbert Minton perfected the art of cheap mass production in the 1840s that tiles became available to the vast majority of people.

CHAPTER TWO

The Rise of the Victorian Tile

Herbert Minton became interested in the lost art of inlaid, or encaustic, tiles around 1828; and although not particularly successful with his experiments in the early stages, he persevered and when Samuel Wright introduced his patent in 1830 for the manufacture of inlaid tiles Minton bought a share in it. Wright's patent was little more than an idea at this stage; he had not perfected the process. The arrangement was that he would take a ten-per-cent royalty on all tiles that Minton sold during the fourteen year life of the patent. The process consisted of impressing a plaster-of-Paris relief into a slab of wet "plastic" clay and filling in the indentations with a liquid clay slip. It was similar to the technique the medieval potters had used. However, differential shrinkage of the clays during firing often led to the inlay falling out or the body cracking and warping, and impurities in the clay gave rise to unpleasant staining. Had it not been for Minton's extraordinary patience, the technique may well have faded into obscurity again. Time and time again he suffered

31. Scrapers, frames and hole punches used in the manufacture of encaustic tiles.

32. Page from the 1844 catalogue of F. St John, G. Barr & Co.

33. Group of encaustic tiles produced by W. Godwin *c* 1853.

34. Encaustic tile. Minton & Co. *c* 1842.

failure, and it was cause for celebration if just a few of the seven hundred tiles fired at each attempt in a small kiln at the china works emerged in a perfect condition. He persevered and in 1835 issued his first catalogue of encaustic tiles which contained sixty-two patterns based on early English medieval designs. In spite of this apparent success the process was extremely slow as each tile was handmade. If tiles were to become a commercial success, then a degree of mechanization had to be introduced. By the time the patent was renewed in 1844, and bought in equal shares by Minton and Fleming St. John, G. Barr & Co. of Worcester, some of the hand work had been replaced by machine, but it was not until 1855 that Samuel Barlow Wright (Samuel Wright's son) and Henry Green invented a mechanical process for the manufacture of plastic-clay encaustic tiles. Despite the advantages of a vastly increased output, many of the other tile manufacturers who were in business by this time resisted mechanization.

An account in the *Hereford Times* (1866) gives a fascinating insight into the production of handmade encaustic tiles at Godwins Encaustic Tile Works. The techniques used there were almost exactly the same as those used by Herbert Minton in the early days, though on a slightly larger scale.

The whole mass of clay is first submitted to what is technically known as "blunging", that is being kept stirred by means of a long slight plank of wood fitted with a transverse handle. When sufficiently "blunged" the mixture is passed to an adjoining tank,

and from thence through "silk" sieves to a third tank, from which, being now of the consistency of thick cream, it is allowed to run off into the long shallow compartments which have hot air flues under them for drying.

The clay is taken, when partially dried, to a room used for the purpose, where it is tempered or beaten by hand on plaster slabs till it is of a proper degree of consistency. This operation is called "wedging", and the clay is delivered to the operators . . . in tolerably sized oblong blocks, a sectional cut across which produces a superficial area of clay a little larger in size than the tile required. The plastic tile is formed of two kinds of clay — that is, the "core" may be of red clay, while it is lapped back and front with a thin layer of grey or any other colour required. The reason for this is, we are told, that it greatly prevents the warping of the article when undergoing the fiery ordeal to which it is afterwards subjected. Each workman has a small plaster disk or table, about the size of, and nearly resembling in shape, the small common cheeses brought to market by country housewives. This disk is made to revolve on a swivel, and the operator laying on it his plaster mould protected by a metal frame, takes a thin outer layer of clay, cut from a lump to his hand, and which he beats out in a trice by the aid of a small flat mallet called a "batter", and with a dexterous slap or two with the open palm of his hand causes it to "bed" well into the block pattern. This done, the superfluous clay is trimmed from the edges. . . . The whole is then surrounded by a deeper metal frame, and the "core" is filled in, pressed down and trimmed out a proper depth by an instrument called a back-cutter, and the whole is ultimately capped with the other outer layer of different coloured clay, the same as the front of the tile is formed. The climax to this part of the process is the placing of a piece of stout leather over the work, and submitting the whole to a powerful squeeze from a lever press. This done, and the superfluous clay again trimmed off, the tile is so far perfect and is carefully eased from the iron mould, but is allowed to stand for some time on that, the plaster mould absorbing the moisture on the plaster cast before it is separated from it, the object being the face of the clay after lying a little, the tile comes away cleaner and more readily. . . . A white colour is run on the face in a liquid form, by the aid of a tiny jug,

35. Encaustic tile. Minton & Co. *c* 1870.
36. Encaustic tile designed by Augustus Pugin for Minton & Co. *c* 1848.
37. Encaustic tile. Minton & Co. *c* 1850.
38. Encaustic tile. Chamberlains (Worcester) *c* 1845.

39. 8-colour encaustic tile. Minton & Co. *c* 1890.

40. 6-colour encaustic tile. Architectural Pottery Co. *c* 1890.
41. 7-colour encaustic tile. Minton & Co. *c* 1885.

after the whole is separated from the mould. When two or more colours are required to be run on in this way each is allowed time to set before the other is applied. The colours are then allowed to set firmly, are roughly cleaned off, and are then laid by face to face to "harden-off", the longer the better, as they then acquire more strength and consistency, and are less liable to injury in the kilns. We saw some splendid medieval tiles made by the plastic process which had been thus hardening for a period of three months. The surface is rendered uniform by being pared off with a knife and afterwards sponged; when to the uninitiated eye they present an incongruous and jumbled mixture of colour in which no pattern is distinguishable. But before being placed in the kilns the surface is damped over again with the sponge, and finally cleaned off with a sharp steel scraper, similar to that used by cabinet-makers in cleaning off their work, when the whole pattern comes out clean and defined. Of course the rapidity with which a workman can turn out this particular description of manufacture depends very much on the elaborateness of the design, but from a dozen and a half to two dozen tiles in a day is about the average. When perfectly manipulated they are placed face to face in pairs, and these pairs are stacked in dozens to harden off; the workrooms being maintained at a uniform degree of temperature in cold weather by the aid of a stove in the centre of each. Each description of tile is finally dried off before baking in a large "drying room", fitted all round with stout shelves purposely for their reception, and heated by means of flues up to about 120 degrees Fahrenheit [49 degrees Centigrade]. Here they are allowed to remain for about a fortnight, after which they are taken away to be burnt.

The figure of two dozen tiles a day seems rather low; other contemporary sources quote from eight or nine dozen, up to as many as two hundred tiles a day.

In 1840 Richard Prosser filed a patent in which he described the making of ceramic buttons from clay dust. Minton realized he could apply the method to the manufacture of tiles and was quick to purchase a share in the patent. Again the idea was extremely simple: dry clay usually called "dust clay" was placed in a mould between two metal plates; under pressure from a screw press, the clay compacted and formed a tile that needed little or no further drying before firing. The earliest of these tiles made by "dust pressing" were plain white wall tiles, which were instantly popular and Minton had difficulty in keeping up with demand. By 1842 he

42. Encaustic tile by the Campbell Brick & Tile Co. *c* 1880.
43. Encaustic tile produced by Robert Minton Taylor *c* 1870.
44. Encaustic tile. Maw & Co. *c* 1850.

25

had sixty presses in operation — mass production had arrived. The method of working was simplicity itself. After ensuring that the plates were clean, the mould was filled with dust clay to an even depth of about ¾ in (19 mm) for a ⅜ in (10 mm) tile, pressure was slowly applied by turning the large wheel at the top of the press in order to expel any air that might be trapped in the powdered clay. The pressure was then taken off and reapplied by forcefully spinning the wheel. Vertical loads in excess of thirty tons were created by the spinning wheel and this caused the dust clay to be compacted into a hard unified tile, which was then ejected from the mould by means of a foot-operated lever. Finally the edges of the tile were smoothed by lightly rubbing with a piece of leather. Later the process was extended to forming embossed tiles simply by replacing one of the flat dies with a relief plate. The plate was made by casting techniques that have changed little to this day. The die which formed the tile back sometimes had the maker's name upon it as well as a raised pattern which formed a key as an aid to fixing. Early tiles made under Prosser's patent have holes in the back like encaustic tiles, as it was thought that dust-pressed tiles also needed them to assist in drying. In fact they were unnecessary and their use was soon discontinued.

Attempts were made to apply the dust-pressing technique to encaustic tiles by using a dust-pressed body inlaid with a liquid slip, but these all proved unsuccessful, mainly because of the differing moisture contents of the clays. However, the problem was solved by Messrs. Boulton & Worthington in 1863 when they patented a process by which encaustic tiles could be made solely from dust clays. The process never ousted the plastic-clay methods and the two usually ran side by side since dust pressing was best applied to simple patterns containing only a few colours; its overriding benefit was the speed at which the tiles could be made, allowing them to become cheaper and available to a much wider market. The quality suffered but as long as the design was not too complex, the results were acceptable. The same article in the *Hereford Times* goes on to describe the process for decorative dust pressing.

45. An early dust-pressed tile. The holes were later dispensed with.

46. Horse head dust-tile press *c* 1880.

The patterns on these compressed tiles are formed of different coloured clays pressed into the face; there are frequently four or five and for each section of the pattern a different plate is required. But, in order to render the thing clearer, we will attempt an illustration, and suppose that the object to be delineated is a "spread" rose. The operator first of all takes a plate with only a circular hole cut through the centre, which is supposed to represent the heart of the flower, and will be formed of yellow clay. By means of a circular hole at each end of his pattern plate the workman fixes it on studs exactly over the disk on which the face of the tile is to be formed, and filling the hole with clay, presses it rightly down by means of a wooden lever at his command. This done, the plate is taken off, and there remains on the disk nothing but a clear round "pip" of clay, any superfluous grains of clay which may have fallen on the disk around the pattern being carefully blown away by the breath of

47. Prosser's patent block-printed tile. Minton & Co. *c* 1850.

a. A bottle oven.

b. Cross-section of a bottle oven. The *hovel* acts as the oven's chimney and protects it from external draughts. The *firemouths*, in which the fires are lit, are located all around the base and the *bags* above them carry the heat into the centre of the oven. The *dampers* are firebrick flaps with which the fireman controls the draught and heat.

the operator. Next the leaves of the flower have to be formed. Another plate having the necessary pattern cut through is fixed on the disk in a similar manner, and the process is repeated with clay powder of another colour, and so on until the leaves, bud, stalk, and every outline is completed, till, as a terminal process, the ground work of the tile is filled in, the latter being effected by encircling the whole pattern in a stout brass collar, filling it with the required powdered clay, and submitting it to the immense pressure of the press before alluded to, when, heigh presto! out comes a tile having each pattern as delicately traced and as nicely blended with the ground work as any painting by hand could effect.

The technique changed little over the years, machinery became more refined, and was capable of producing more tiles, but overall, the basic principles still applied.

Before being taken to the bottle oven which was a 70-ft (21-m) high, brick, bottle-shaped structure reinforced with iron straps, the tiles were packed face to face in fire-clay containers called "saggars", which were about the size of a Victorian footbath. The full saggars weighing 56 lb (25 kg) were taken to the oven by the "placer", who normally carried the saggar on his head. Inside the oven, the saggars were "placed" one on top of the other from floor to ceiling, well in towards the centre using the base of the topmost saggar as a cover for the one beneath. This ensured that no impurities could enter and damage the tiles. An average bottle oven could hold two thousand saggars containing some twenty-five tons of tiles. After further preparations, the door was bricked up and the firing commenced which, depending on the tiles being fired, lasted from two to five days. The temperatures ranged from 1,000 to 1,250 degrees Centigrade. The most responsible job in the whole tile works belonged to the "fireman" who usually remained with the oven throughout the firing, and who ensured that all the conditions were met for a successful completion. It was a job that

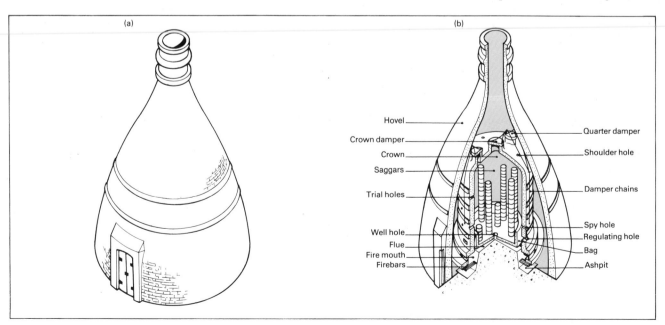

could only be done by informed guesswork and experience, and a skilled fireman was greatly prized by his employer. After two or three days, the oven cooled sufficiently for the tiles to be "drawn", but the contents were still hot enough to impart a nasty burn. When quite cool, those tiles to be glazed were carried to the enamelling department on long, narrow wooden planks called wareboards. In the enamelling department the glaze was brushed on and dried almost immediately, after which the tile was taken to the Glost kiln for its second firing. The Glost kilns were arched ovens of no great depth in a rectangular brick structure. The tiles were stacked in these ovens face upwards, on small refractory tripods whose legs stood clear of the tiles so that as the placing progressed, the tiles were laid clear of each other, preventing the glaze from being damaged by contact with the tile above. After firing for about twelve hours at about 700 degrees Centigrade, the kiln was allowed to cool and finally drawn.

Over the years tile-making techniques varied but they were all expansions on the methods described above. The main variation in the production of tiles lay in the decoration, and here the scope was virtually unlimited. By using the right combination of manufacturing technique and design the tile makers were able to offer the Victorian and Edwardian public an unsurpassable array of tiles of every description.

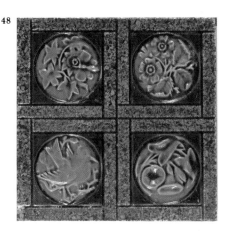

48. Mottled effect moulded tile with 2 different clays by W. Godwin, 1880.

Decorative Processes

With the exception of unglazed encaustic tiles, each tile had to be fired at least twice; firstly to make the tile biscuit, and secondly to apply the glaze and any further decoration. At first the colours and glazes were compounded on the manufacturers' own premises, but as the industry developed, firms like Wengers supplied most of the colours and glazes in a pre-prepared form. There were a limited number of techniques that could be applied to the basic tile body; it was either flat, inlaid, or had some kind of relief impressed upon it. Leaving aside inlaid or encaustic decoration which has already been discussed, there was only one main variable in the manufac-

49. Design for one of a series of plaques by E. Hammond c 1875.
50. Majolica tile subsequently taken from the design on Fig. 49 c 1880.

51. Heavily moulded tile, majolica glazed, from a series of 6 tiles, *The Hanging of the Crane* by Longfellow. Maw & Co. *c* 1875.
52. Plaster original used in the manufacture of Fig. 51.
53. Moulded majolica tile in 3-colour glazes. Corn Bros. *c* 1895.

54. Barbotine tile. Sherwin & Cotton *c* 1890.

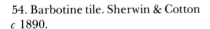

ture of the tile biscuit which affected the decoration, namely the colour of the clay. Most tiles were of a single colour though a very striking mottled effect could be achieved by combining two or more different coloured clays. This was particularly effective when used in conjunction with an embossed pattern and coloured majolica glazes. The more common methods of decoration are listed below, but very rarely were they used in isolation and most tiles display a combination of techniques.

The Glazes

The glaze is a glass-like coating, completely impervious (unless crazed), which was largely responsible for the acceptance of tiles as an aid to cleanliness. In the 1850s Leon Arnoux of Mintons pioneered the use of majolica glazes, both transparent and opaque. These glazes, which were made by adding different metallic oxides to a basic glaze composition, looked most effective when applied to embossed tiles; and different effects could be achieved by the careful positioning of the tile during firing. For instance if the tile was laid absolutely flat, the glaze would pond in the lower areas appearing darker than the adjacent raised areas. Alternatively if the tile was tilted, the glaze would run to one side and create a gradation of tone across the whole tile. Different coloured glazes could be used on the same tile, and by applying them with a brush instead of the usual dipping, they could be made to run into each other or kept separate by the contours of the pattern. It was also

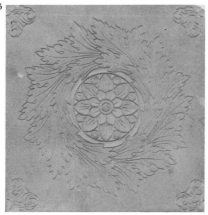

possible to apply different coloured glazes with repeated firings, a new colour being added each time.

Flat tiles, decorated by one of the other techniques, were usually covered with a colourless or transparent glaze which benefited the whole design by bringing out the colours in the decoration and in the tile body itself. Even basic faults were put to decorative purposes. The most common was crazing caused by excessive contraction of the glaze relative to the tile body. If the crazing was caused deliberately, it was possible to fill in the cracks with a contrasting colour and apply a further coat of glaze to create a Chinese decorative effect. Until 1900 most of the glazes were lead based but with the growing awareness of the threat to health, new, safer glazes were gradually introduced, but in general these lacked the depth and lustre of the old lead glazes.

Incised Decoration

In this method of decoration the design was incised in an unfired plastic-clay tile. This was usually done by hand but later tiles were made by impressing a metal die into clay giving a similar effect. Sometimes the incision was filled with coloured stains to highlight the design. The tiles were usually left unglazed.

Sgraffito

This was an extension of incised decoration. A tile biscuit was coated in a contrasting slip which when dry could be scratched through with a pointed tool to reveal the colour of the tile body below. If areas of slip were removed rather than lines, the technique was known as sgraffiato.

Barbotine

Barbotine was a hand painting method based on oil painting techniques. Coloured slips were painted directly onto the biscuit-fired tile, which may have been given a layer of slip beforehand. Minimal use of the painted slip gave the best results, and if a

55. Unglazed incised tile. Maw & Co. *c* 1880.
56. Beautifully glazed majolica tile. Corn Bros. *c* 1900.
57. Hand-painted tile. By W. B. Simpson & Sons *c* 1885.

30

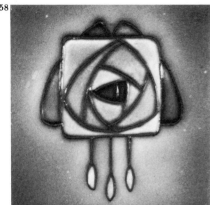

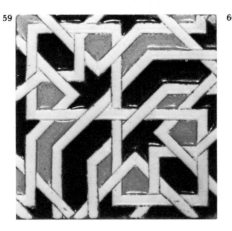

58. Tube-lined Art Nouveau tile produced by H. Richards *c* 1905.
59. Spanish *de cuenca* tile *c* 1860.
60. Machine-made derivative of *de cuerda seca*. Maw & Co. *c* 1885.

greater relief was required, it could be obtained by using a slightly stiffer modelled slip. Later floor tiles were printed using a similar technique but they were extremely susceptible to wear. Barbotine was sometimes called slip painting.

Pâte sur Pâte

This type of decoration on tiles is rare and was only practised by skilled exponents of art, notably Louis Marc Solon who, at Mintons, perfected the technique and successfully applied it to the decoration of porcelain. A shallow relief was gradually built up by applying repeated layers of thin white slip to a darker base. Tonal variation was achieved by the different thicknesses of slip allowing the darker base to show through to a greater or lesser degree.

Tube Lining

This distinctive technique owes much to the Spanish *de cuenca* method of decoration. *De cuenca* (bowl) and *de cuerda seca* (dry cord) are traditional Moorish techniques used to separate adjacent areas of glazes. *De cuerda seca* involved lightly incising a design on a plastic-clay tile, after which the resulting troughs were filled with a greasy substance which prevented the coloured glazes spilling over into each other, and created a shallow relief over the tile surface. *De cuenca* is the exact opposite and the incised lines were replaced by sharp ridges formed by depressing adjacent areas of the soft clay tile, causing a raised seam to be formed which separated the glazes.

In tube lining, areas of coloured glazes making up the design were kept separate by raised seams of a contrasting slip piped onto the tile over a design outlined by pouncing. The tube line could be applied to a tile biscuit or an unfired tile, and the coloured glazes added at the same time or afterwards depending on the desired effect. Great care had to be exercised when matching the tube-line slip with the tile body, otherwise it was liable to fall off after firing. Unfortunately these tiles were relatively expensive and in order to make them available to the popular market the technique was adapted to machine production simply by making a metal die from which tiles could be pressed in imitation of the real thing. Tube

31

61

62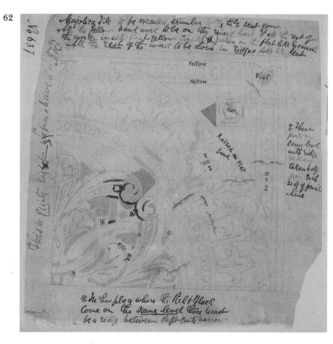

63

64

65

66

67

68

66. Hand-decorated barbotine tile.
Sherwin & Cotton *c* 1890.
67. Hand-painted on Minton & Co.
blank *c* 1855.
68. Transfer-printed and
hand-painted floral tile. J. H. Barratt
& Co. *c* 1880.

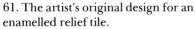

61. The artist's original design for an
enamelled relief tile.
62. Working drawing which details
every aspect of the modelling and
decoration.
63. Plaster-of-Paris master from which
the metal die is made.
64. The finished tile. No. 637 in the
Maw catalogue.
65. Unique hand-painted panel signed
but unattributed *c* 1890.

69-71. Unsigned hand-painted
underglaze *c* 1880.

lining was at its most popular in the Art Nouveau period, though it was well established long before then, particularly in mural painting.

Hand Painting

A great many tiles and panels were produced by hand painting a design or picture on a tile biscuit, with or without a covering slip. A thorough understanding of the behaviour of ceramic colours was essential, since the true colours did not emerge until after the glazing and firing. Transfer-printed designs were often coloured by hand as a substitute for colour printing but often the results were slipshod, with the colours overreaching the confines of the design. Overglaze painting was popular as a greater range of colours was available. Though they lacked the brilliance of underglaze colours they could be fired at a much lower temperature and remained virtually the same after firing. Tiles were often

69

70

71

33

sold with a pre-decorated underglaze border pattern with the intention that the purchaser should apply his or her own overglaze enamels to complete the tile. These are particularly common in fireplace surrounds.

72. "Jack and Jill". Hand-painted overglaze to a design by Walter Crane. Mintons China Works *c* 1880.
73-74. Transfer-printed and hand-painted tiles. Minton Hollins *c* 1875.

Transfer Printing

This was the most commonly applied process. In its most common form, an etched or engraved copper plate was carefully inked with a mixture of ceramic colour, linseed oil and a little resin or gum to help in the adhesion of the print. After removing the excess colour from the plate a thin sheet of transfer paper, previously damped and sized (usually in a soap solution), was rolled firmly down onto the plate. When the paper was dry, it was carefully peeled away, trimmed and applied face down onto the tile surface. After several hours the paper was soaked off, leaving the transferred image behind. To ensure good adhesion of the print and to evaporate off any remaining oils, the decorated tile biscuit was given a low-temperature firing, followed, after any further decoration, by glazing and firing. At first the printing was done on crude, hand-operated printing tables, and the drying carried out in front of a fire; but later, steam-heated printing tables enabled the whole operation to be carried out more efficiently. Later still, completely automated printing machines were introduced. While most companies had their own printing department, ancillary firms who

75-78. A selection of typical transfer-printed tiles *c* 1870-85: (75) Maw & Co. (76) Mintons China Works. (77) Minton Hollins. (78) Wedgwood.

specialized in transfer printing supplied pre-made transfers to the tile makers. Most of these designs were available to anybody and it was common to find the same design duplicated by several manufacturers.

The technique of block printing, introduced at Mintons by Collins and Reynolds in 1848, enabled areas of different colour to be laid down by transfer printing and was used extensively by Mintons to produce their multicoloured picture tiles in the 1870s. Prior to this, block printing had been used on tiles designed by Augustus Pugin for the smoking room in the House of Commons. The process involved cutting a flat metal plate to produce raised areas which corresponded to the use of one colour in the design. Further blocks were cut for each of the other colours, and, in turn, all the colours were printed in register onto a transfer paper. Lithographic printing was also used by the turn of the century, and eventually replaced block printing altogether. Very much later, silk-screen printing was applied to tile production and found favour with firms like Maw & Co. and Carter & Co.

Aerography

In its simplest form aerography consisted of spraying colour through a stencil onto the face of the tile. Several designs by C. H. Temple of Maw & Co. were produced by aerography, and Carter & Co. also undertook some experimental work of this kind.

35

79. Transfer-printed tile produced by Ollivant *c* 1890.

80. Block-printed tile with further hand colouring. Minton Hollins *c* 1860.

81. Tile with machine-applied relief decoration. Maw & Co. *c* 1890.

82. Same design as Fig. 79 after hand colouring. Produced by Ollivant *c* 1890.

83. Hand-painted overglaze with applied gold leaf decoration. Copeland 1880.

84. Hand-painted underglaze *c* 1885.
8 in × 8 in (20 cm × 20 cm) tile.
85. Moulded tile. J. H. Barratt & Co.
c 1900.
86. Block-printed tile. Maw & Co.
c 1880.
87. Stencilled and aerographed design
by C. H. Temple. Maw & Co. *c* 1890.

Metallic Decoration

Gold, platinum and silver were the only metals that could resist the intense heat of firing and remain in a metallic state. They were sometimes used in leaf form as underglaze decoration. Tiles decorated in this manner were very expensive and were only produced to special order for those who could afford them. A more common method of using gold was to apply it as gilding over the glaze and many Copeland tiles display this feature.

Lustres

Lustre decoration, an imitation of the Persian and Moorish wares of antiquity, rapidly gained popularity in the 1880s and '90s, mainly due to the efforts of William De Morgan who devoted a great deal of energy to its reintroduction. The decoration was created by refiring at low temperature a tile whose glaze was rich in metallic oxide, or which had been coated with a solution of the oxide, in an atmosphere containing impurities, known as a reducing atmosphere. The effect of the reducing atmosphere was to remove the oxygen from the metallic oxide leaving behind a thin layer of metal which shone with irridescence. Absolute precision in all aspects of firing was vital as even a small variation in technique could result in failure. The most commonly used lustres were of silver and copper: the former gave a metallic appearance with a yellow sheen, and the latter a rich, metallic, ruby red.

Architectural and Domestic Tiling

Encaustic tiles rapidly gained popularity during the early years of the Gothic revival when the Victorian fervour for the rehabilitation of old churches and cathedrals was at its height, and with the new industrial wealth it was not long before every important public building boasted magnificent tiled floors, corridors and pavements, often designed by the architect responsible for the rest of the building. As a flooring material tiles were ideal; they were extremely durable, easy to clean and maintain, and were highly decorative. They were also possessed of another important virtue — they were frost and weather resistant — and before long their use was extended to include a multitude of external applications. Encaustic tiles found their way into greenhouses, conservatories, footpaths, porches; and onto the walls of buildings as name plates commemorative plaques and street signs. They were even used to decorate gravestones.

Tiles for use as external decoration was by no means a new idea. The Greek and Roman civilizations had used glazed bricks extensively; fifteenth century Florence had seen the rise of terracotta and glazed faience, some of the best examples of which

88

88. 18th-century bath. Carshalton, Surrey.

89. Panel by J.S. Bontal for a butcher's shop, Chiswick, London.

90. Hand-painted butcher's shop panel. Corn Bros. *c* 1900.

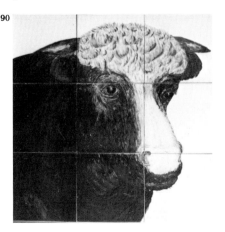

originated from the workshops of Della Robbia, a source of much inspiration to the late Victorian tile makers; and Eastern cultures had utilized glazed decoration on their minarets and domes. All these influences led designers like William De Morgan, Halsey Ricardo and Walter Crane to advocate the use of colourful glazed ceramics for external decoration. Most of the dust-pressed tiles, however, simply could not stand up to the rigours of the northern climate. It was vital that the tiles be impermeable, otherwise a tile-clad building would quickly become an eyesore as the glaze crazed and admitted dirt; and even more important, would become a danger as frost and the elements loosened tiles from its façade. As the rate of building in Victorian England increased and the new middle classes grew with the expanding towns, there arose an insatiable demand for a cheap, decorative and functional material with which to clad a building. If tiles were unsuitable, then terracotta was the next best thing. Despite the difficulty of manufacture, the material was far more economic than stone, though just as strong, and was often used as part of the structure. Although dirt and grime tended to accumulate on it, it resisted corrosion, and could be mass produced and moulded into an infinite variety of shapes.

Doulton & Co. continued to research into the architectural possibilities of glazed ceramics and in the late 1870s came up with Doultonware, an extremely hard, salt-glazed material which could withstand the most violent extremes of weather. Despite the popularity of terracotta, it was no match for Doultonware, which was self-cleaning, when it rained, and was available in a greater variety of colours. Other manufacturers followed Doulton's lead and began producing architectural faience for use on the façades of pubs, shops, hotels and other buildings where it was important to create a clean, inviting appearance. One of the major arguments against the widespread use of glazed tiles and faience was their highly reflective surface which caused annoyance not only to pedestrian traffic but to horses. Doulton's answer was Carraraware which had more of a lustrous sheen than a high glaze.

Tile panels often advertised the purpose of the building or the trade that was carried on within it. The largest buyers of architectural ceramics were the breweries whose use of ceramic decoration extended from ornate pub frontages to the bars within, which were very often tiled from floor to ceiling with elaborate majolica-glazed dados and hand-painted panels.

With the introduction of various health acts tiles were used extensively in hospitals, dairies and other places of food preparation. At first the tiles tended to be plain white, but soon the wards were brightened with the addition of colourful panels made by Doulton, Pilkingtons and Carter. An account of the uses of tiles by William Blake in *Ceramic Art* (1875) described contemporary philosophy regarding tiles as an aid to hygiene:

Besides the use of the glazed and enamelled tiles in mural decoration for dados, panels, etc., they are especially applicable, and are largely used abroad, for lining the walls of dairies (the

39

dairy farmers finding them superior for cleanliness and keeping the milk pure), for larders, kitchens, around sinks and cooking-ranges, in bath-rooms, water-closets, and in stables. For such places the six-inch plain white glazed tile is in general use. Another very important application of wall-tiles is in hospitals, for completely lining the walls of wards for fever patients. The new St. Thomas hospitals (erected in London opposite the Houses of Parliament) have the fever wards lined with six-inch white glazed tiles, which, it is believed, will prevent the absorption of the germs of disease which it is well known penetrate porous plaster walls, and are even absorbed by bricks, so that after a time whole wards of hospitals and entire buildings become unfit for occupation. The same is true of rooms in dwellings, hotels and dormitories in colleges. An impervious tile-wall, which can be thoroughly cleaned by wiping with a sponge, is a great sanitary improvement, and deserves the attention of physicians and architects. A thoroughly vitrified body like porcelain, would be better for the purpose than a porous earthenware base with a glazed surface, though the latter would, no doubt, be far better than even the hardest painted plaster wall.

Another important use of the plain white glazed, or enamelled tiles, is as reflectors in lining dark passages, staircases and entrances, especially to basements, or wherever there is liability to dampness or a smoky atmosphere. They are largely used about the stations of the underground railway in London, particularly around the window-openings, or wherever light is admitted through thick walls.

By the mid-1870s wall tiles had become as indispensable as floor tiling, and no self-respecting council or private landlord would allow his property to be devoid of this novel form of ceramic decoration, and so tiles were used increasingly, not because of their hygenic attributes, but for their decorative effect. The fashion

91. Charing Cross Hospital, London 1881.
92. Gentleman's lavatory. Philharmonic Public House, Liverpool *c* 1899.

93. Patent mosaic floors from a Maw & Co. catalogue page *c* 1894.

94. Gledhow Hall, Leeds. Faience tiling produced by Burmantofts 1885.

95. Lloyds Bank fountain, The Strand, London. Doulton 1883.

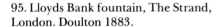

quickly spread to the homes of the middle classes who were able to purchase tiles at a reasonable price. As mass-production techniques improved, even the poorest-paid worker could afford tiled decoration in his home and Victorian England embarked on a domestic fashion which was to sweep the Empire, and break through all rank and class barriers.

As the cities and towns prospered, new housing was built to keep pace with their increasing populations. The endless new rows of anonymous terraced houses and cottages threatened to drown their occupants in a sea of obscurity. Decorative tiles, however, helped preserve each house's individual identity. The porchway became the focal point and in the richer areas was decorated with beautifully executed tile panels in a majolica surround, while the poorer districts made do with simple, plain coloured tiles, enlivened with a majolica moulding. As manufacturing techniques improved and tiles became more weather resistant, it was quite usual for small panels of decorated tiles to be set into the front wall of a house around the windows or as a single course midway up the house.

Encaustic and plain coloured floor tiles were an ideal replacement for wooden skirting boards which had been rotted by rising damp. For the same reason tiles were often used on window-sills. But it was the walls of hallways that offered the best opportunity to display one's good taste, and it was here that embossed majolica tiles really came into their own. The dados very often lined the walls of the staircase and continued along the upper storeys.

In Victorian times fireplaces were mass produced in cast iron at an unprecedented rate and tiles were fixed within the framework of the surround to form the familiar "tile register" fireplace. They were also "slabbed" to build up a complete fire surround in tiles, the fire being contained in a free-standing grate. Slabbed tiles were pre-fixed at the factory to a firm base, usually slate or concrete, so the resulting panel could be cemented in place on site. This technique was commonly applied to fireplaces and hearths since it meant that the whole thing could be assembled from only three or four pre-tiled pieces, saving time and money. Other small panels for use in porches were very often slabbed and used in conjunction with individual tiles. Later on, firms like Doulton were able to supply complete, factory-assembled tiled fireplaces which were delivered in one piece ready for fixing. As the fireplace was regarded as the centre of the room great care had to be exercised in choosing the tiles; they were always strongly representative of the owner's idea of good taste. Tiled stoves were also popular and were used where a fireplace was impractical or unnecessary: in the hall for example, or in changing rooms, or to add a further touch of luxury in the bathroom.

The new craze for bathrooms provided yet another outlet for the tile manufacturers whose products were considered ideal for the hot, steamy environment, and while not everyone wanted to go to the extremes of a complete bathroom fitted out in ceramics, which Burmantofts undertook to do for a "moderate" sum, firms, like

41

96. Suggested uses for decorative tilework. Maw & Co. *c* 1885.

Doulton, that specialized in sanitary fittings benefited greatly and supplied baths complete with tiled surrounds. They also sold elaborate "lavatories" — complete pieces of furniture which included a washbasin, mirrors, cupboards and a tiled splashback. For the average household the wash-stand served as the only washing facility and here tiles were used to good effect, glued to a cardboard backing or screwed through the corners onto a wood support within a wooden frame. Tiles even found their way into furniture. Tables of all kinds were tiled, as were chairs, stools, overmantles, and occasionally sideboards and cupboards. Tiled plant stands also came into vogue since they would not be damaged by water, though they were susceptible to wear from the base of the

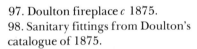

97. Doulton fireplace *c* 1875.
98. Sanitary fittings from Doulton's catalogue of 1875.

jardinières placed on top of them. Flower boxes suffered no such wear as the plant pots were placed inside. An obvious use for an individual tile was as a teapot stand and these could be purchased ready made with factory-applied ceramic feet, or one could buy a simple wire frame and fix it to the tile at home. Not surprisingly, tiles were collected and displayed in frames as pictures and this accounts for the high proportion of seemingly unused tiles which are around today.

With the change in interior decor that accompanied a rise in living standards, the dados were gradually removed and replaced with wallpaper, the wash-stands disappeared, tiled furniture went out of fashion, the old cast-iron fireplaces were pulled out and replaced by "modern" slabbed fire surrounds.

The English Tile Overseas

The earliest tiles to be exported from England were from the Liverpool workshops of John Sadler and Guy Green whose printed tiles were shipped from the port in large numbers, and even today can be found in remote corners of the United States. With the advent of mass production in the nineteenth century Britain already had an established export market to the United States; the

MALKIN, EDGE, & Co.'S PATENT ENCAUSTIC TILES,
BURSLEM,
ART-PAINTED TILES FOR HEARTHS, GRATE CHEEKS, &c.

No. 294.   No. 295.   No. 296.

6 × 6 Tiles   6 × 6 Tiles   8 × 8 Tiles

No. 297.   No. 298.   No. 299.

6 × 6 Tiles   6 × 6 Tiles   8 × 8 Tiles

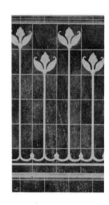

British Empire was expanding; colonial offices and government buildings were being built all over the world; foreign heads of state vied with each other to create tiled schemes that were bigger and better than those of their neighbours; but perhaps the biggest factor in the commercial overseas success of the British tile industry lay in its performance at the major international exhibitions. After the 1851 Great Exhibition in London, not a year passed without some showing of the prowess of the industrialized nations. No self-respecting tile company could afford to miss these events. Maw & Co. won at least ten medals by 1880 in the International Exhibitions of London 1862, Oporto 1865, Dublin 1866, Paris 1867, Dublin 1872, London 1874, Paris 1875, Philadelphia 1876, Sydney 1879 and Melbourne 1880.

Every large tile company saw to it that they had at least one agent in the principal cities of the major continents. In New York for instance were agents Alfred Boote for Mintons China Works, Miller & Coates for Minton Hollins, Canover & Co. for the Campbell Brick and Tile Co., and Robert Rossman and William H. Jackson Co. for Maw. In the 1880s, with the worldwide demand for tiles reaching almost epidemic proportions, the number of appointed agents grew — Maw & Co. had agents in Europe, Canada, the United States, South Africa, Australia, New Zealand, India, Japan and China.

If the English seem to have had it all their own way at the start, by 1890 thriving tile industries in the United States, Germany, France and Australia offered serious competition, but though English trade suffered in wall tiling, no other country could

99. Malkin Edge & Co. catalogue page
c 1890.

100. Dado tiling from Gibbons Hinton
c 1900.

101

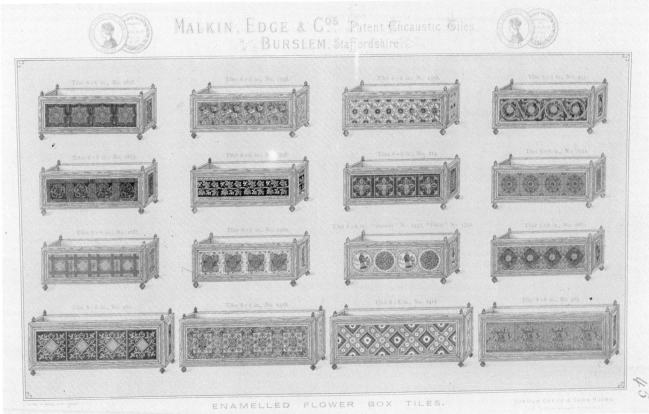

MALKIN, EDGE & C?s Patent Encaustic Tiles.
BURSLEM, Staffordshire.

ENAMELLED FLOWER BOX TILES.

102. Flower boxes. Malkin Edge & Co. catalogue *c* 1890.

101 and 103. Tiles were often incorporated into chairs and cabinets. Tile in chair by Mintons China Works *c* 1878. The one in the cabinet is by Doulton *c* 1880.

compete with the expertise of the English when it came to encaustic floor tiles. However, the promise of a freer working environment tempted many leading English designers and craftsmen overseas to the American and Australian industries. Leon Solon worked with the American Encaustic Tile Co., and George Cartlidge, whose portrait tiles of American statesmen were so popular, worked with the Alhambra Tile Co. in Newport, Kentucky, and the Fine Art Ceramic Co., Indianapolis. One company, the International Tile and Trim Co. of Brooklyn, was financed by English money and run by English craftsmen who had come from Maw & Co.

Before long the American companies were establishing agents in this country, as were the Australians, Germans and French. English companies found they were competing on home ground with tile industries whose wares were substantially different from their own. Villeroy & Boch, the old-established German company, had agents in Hatton Garden, London, from where it sold mosaics, individual tiles and panels in addition to a wide range of earthenware and other ceramic goods; and Montereau L. M. & Cie, Creil, of France also had a strong foothold in England. Though these competing industries damaged the English trade to some extent, trade throughout the rest of the world was so good that the effect was hardly noticeable. The industry ultimately did suffer at the height of Art Nouveau, when the Continental tiles were generally preferred to their English counterparts. The eventual decline in the decorated-tile industry, however, was experienced by companies the world over.

45

CHAPTER THREE

Principal Tile Manufacturers

The Minton Tile Companies

The average builder of the 1870s could well be forgiven for shaking his head in utter bewilderment when it came to selecting tiles. Not only were there well over a hundred different companies to choose from, each of which produced an enormous range, but three of them seemed to be using the same name — Minton. If this caused chaos in 1870, then it is no wonder that the name of Minton on tiles causes such confusion today.

When Herbert Minton was sixteen he became a travelling representative for the growing pottery business started in Stoke-on-Trent by his father, Thomas Minton. In 1817 he and his brother Thomas William were taken into partnership. When, in 1830, Samuel Wright introduced his patent for the manufacture of ornamental tiles, Minton, who had been experimenting in the same field, bought a share in it, and began to perfect the technique, which at this stage was really little more than an idea. Despite many failures in the early years, Minton continued his experiments, to final success.

Minton's early successes were largely due to his adopting Wedgwood's maxim of selling directly to the aristocracy. It was not long before he executed his first royal commission — a pavement for Queen Victoria at Osborne House on the Isle of Wight in 1844. Soon commissions from the Church who needed tiles for the restoration of its cathedrals and building of churches were forthcoming; Augustus Pugin and his contemporaries used Minton tiles almost as fast as he could make them.

In 1845 Michael Daintry Hollins, a nephew of Minton's wife, joined the firm. With his knowledge of chemistry he was a considerable asset to Minton and some of Hollins's glazes are still unsurpassed. On his joining the firm the business was split into two quite independent departments: china, and tile manufacture. The china side of the business continued as Minton & Co. and the tile business became known as Minton Hollins & Co. (though floor tiles were still marked Minton & Co.). By 1846 Samuel Barlow Wright — son of the original patentee — had become a partner in the

104. Encaustic tile. Minton & Co. *c* 1850.
105. *Sporting*. Mintons China Works *c* 1886.

THE MINTON TILE COMPANIES

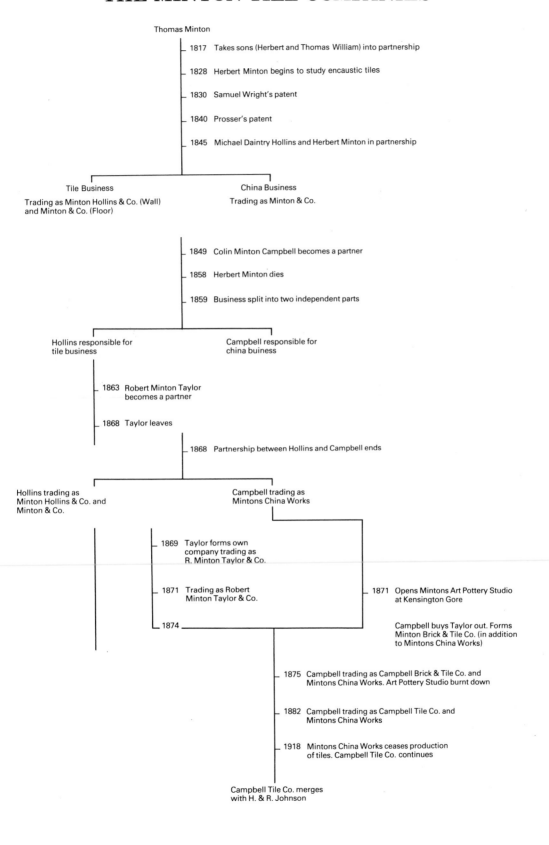

Thomas Minton

1817 Takes sons (Herbert and Thomas William) into partnership

1828 Herbert Minton begins to study encaustic tiles

1830 Samuel Wright's patent

1840 Prosser's patent

1845 Michael Daintry Hollins and Herbert Minton in partnership

Tile Business
Trading as Minton Hollins & Co. (Wall)
and Minton & Co. (Floor)

China Business
Trading as Minton & Co.

1849 Colin Minton Campbell becomes a partner

1858 Herbert Minton dies

1859 Business split into two independent parts

Hollins responsible for
tile business

Campbell responsible for
china buiness

1863 Robert Minton Taylor
becomes a partner

1868 Taylor leaves

1868 Partnership between Hollins and Campbell ends

Hollins trading as
Minton Hollins & Co. and
Minton & Co.

Campbell trading as
Mintons China Works

1869 Taylor forms own
company trading as
R. Minton Taylor & Co.

1871 Trading as Robert
Minton Taylor & Co.

1871 Opens Mintons Art Pottery Studio
at Kensington Gore

1874

Campbell buys Taylor out. Forms
Minton Brick & Tile Co. (in addition
to Mintons China Works)

1875 Campbell trading as Campbell Brick & Tile Co. and
Mintons China Works. Art Pottery Studio burnt down

1882 Campbell trading as Campbell Tile Co. and
Mintons China Works

1918 Mintons China Works ceases production
of tiles. Campbell Tile Co. continues

Campbell Tile Co. merges
with H. & R. Johnson

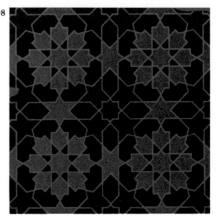

company, followed in 1849 by Colin Minton Campbell — yet another of Minton's nephews. Herbert Minton and his partners consolidated their position with two important developments: firstly the introduction of majolica glazes, and secondly the new block technique for transfer printing.

When Herbert Minton died in 1858, Hollins and Campbell entered into a new agreement whereby Hollins took complete charge of the tile business, and Campbell ran the china works. Under this agreement the tile business prospered and Hollins took on a partner in 1863 — Robert Minton Taylor — who later left in 1868 just before the partnership between Hollins and Campbell terminated. Hollins was left owning the tile business, and Campbell became the sole proprietor of the china business. If Hollins had rested content with this arrangement the firm of Minton Hollins & Co. may well have had no further competition from Minton & Co. — or Mintons China Works as they now were called. But instead, Hollins insisted on Campbell paying for the equipment and stock at the china works, which eventually he did; and with the money, Hollins constructed himself a new purpose-built tile factory. However, with his "newly purchased equipment" Campbell began producing tiles on a large scale (he had been producing majolica tiles in limited numbers for some time). So in 1868 there were two completely separate and independent companies: Minton Hollins & Co. producing wall and floor tiles, and Mintons China Works manufacturing wall tiles only. To further complicate matters,

106-107. Embossed in majolica enamels. Mintons China Works c 1880, 8 in × 8 in (20 cm × 20 cm).
108. Block-printed. Mintons China Works c 1880, 8 in × 8 in (20cm × 20cm).

109. Block-printed. Mintons China Works c 1885.

48

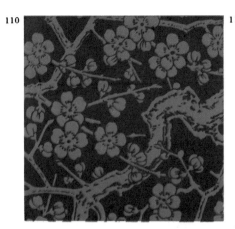

110. Block-printed. Mintons China Works *c* 1880, 8 in × 8 in (20 cm × 20 cm).
111. Hand-painted. Mintons China Works *c* 1870, 8 in × 8 in (20 cm × 20 cm).
112. Hand-painted to a design by Pugin. Minton & Co. *c* 1850, 12 in × 12 in (30 cm × 30 cm).

Robert Minton Taylor set himself up in 1869 trading as R. Minton Taylor & Co., capitalizing on the reputation of the two already established companies.

A series of law suits were instigated by Hollins with the object of clarifying the position as to the use of the name "Minton", and, if possible, to put the others out of business. The outcome was that all three continued in business, though Robert Minton Taylor had to trade under his full name and Hollins gained exclusive rights to the titles Minton Hollins and Co. and Minton & Co., leaving Campbell to trade as Mintons China Works. Campbell bought Taylor out in 1874 and formed the Minton Brick and Tile Co. (in addition to Mintons China Works). Further law suits followed, resulting in the

113-114. *Views*. Mintons China Works *c* 1885. 113 is by William Wise, and 114 by L. T. Swetnam.

formation of the Campbell Brick and Tile Co., owned by Campbell and run by Taylor.

Though Mintons China Works produced by far the largest number of picture tiles, Minton Hollins captured the overall tile market with designs aimed more at the working population than those of their rivals.

Mintons China Works and the Art Pottery Studio

In 1871 Mintons opened the Art Pottery Studio in Kensington Gore under the directorship of W. S. Coleman in response to an increasing number of commissions resulting from the tiling that had just been completed at the South Kensington Museum. The studio complemented its parent company admirably and in addition to providing a creative environment in which artists and designers could work on individual tiles and panels, it provided the factory in Stoke with a continual stream of new designs that could be adapted for mass production. During the short life of the studio, which burnt down in 1875, it produced large numbers of tiles, plaques and other ornamental wares and became something of a show-case for the best of contemporary ceramic design. But the great majority of the China Works' tiles were produced by "in house" designers.

In 1877 the China Works took out a patent for its new Morocco surface, which was suitable for either hand painting or printing. The contemporary press hailed the leather-like surface as a triumph, since it eliminated reflection. Few tiles are found with this surface, however, and those that are tend to be large hand-painted slabs used in architectural rather than domestic applications. Some Copeland tiles are known with this finish. It could be that they are experimental tiles bought by Campbell to see how his patent would perform on other tiles; or that Copeland bought rights to the patent; or, more likely, that Copeland had some of their tiles coated with the new surface which were later decorated at their factory.

115. Mintons China Works c 1875. From an earlier design by Augustus Pugin.

116. *Days of the Week*. Mintons China Works c 1880.
117. *Watteau Subjects*. Mintons China Works c 1870.
118. *Elfins*. Mintons China Works c 1874.

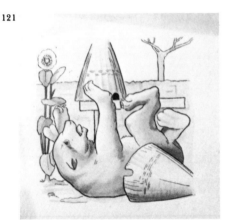

119. Mintons China Works *c* 1880. This design was also used by Steele & Wood.
120. Rare Mintons China Works tile *c* 1890.
121. Original designs for *Fables* by Henk. Mintons China Works *c* 1882.
122. "Willow Pattern". Mintons China Works *c* 1885.
123. Transfer-printed tile. Mintons China Works *c* 1870-85.

Probably more than any other factory, Mintons China Works utilized its designs to the full and many of its printed and hand-painted designs were later used as modelled majolica tiles. An excellent example of this is the series of musicians designed by Edward Hammond at the Art Pottery Studio which was first made as hand-painted plaques and later produced in majolica (see Fig. 50).

By 1900 the tide was turning against picture tiles in favour of Art Nouveau work, and so the China Works decided to devote its energies elsewhere and began to run down the tile business. By 1918 all tile production ceased, and in the light of the slump in the tile industry that followed, the decision was a wise one.

124

124. Panel painted at the Kensington Gore Studio on tile blanks by R. Minton Taylor *c* 1873.

Robert Minton Taylor

Robert Minton Taylor was in business for six years and yet relatively few of his tiles survive. Sir Edward Poynter used his tiles for the Grill Room at the South Kensington Museum, and Mintons' Art Pottery Studio used his tile blanks extensively. Probably through his connections there, several artists, including Stacey Marks, designed and painted tiles for him.

In 1874 he sold out to Campbell who formed the Minton Brick and Tile Co.

Campbell Brick and Tile Co.

When Campbell formed the Minton Brick and Tile Co., Hollins again resorted to legal action to try and stop the new business. The result of the action prohibited Campbell from using the name Minton in any connection other than Mintons China Works. Hollins's triumph was short lived, however, for Campbell simply changed the name of the company to the Campbell Brick and Tile Co. Very quickly the new company established itself as a supplier of high-quality plain and encaustic floor tiles and pavements. After 1882, when it became the Campbell Tile Co., it produced an

125-126. Patterns for the *Old English Sports and Games*. Mintons China Works *c* 1882.
127. Original design for *Scenes in the Hunting Field*. Mintons China Works *c* 1882.

125

126

127

52

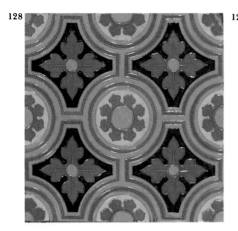

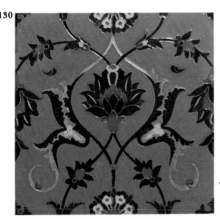

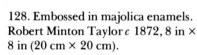

128. Embossed in majolica enamels. Robert Minton Taylor *c* 1872, 8 in × 8 in (20 cm × 20 cm).

129. *Children's Games.* Minton Hollins *c* 1875.

130. Embossed in majolica enamels. Mintons China Works *c* 1880, 8 in × 8 in (20 cm × 20 cm).

increasing range of majolica and transfer-printed tiles for use in flower boxes, fireplaces, walls, pilasters and other architectural work — a field in which it excelled. Architects found the scale drawings of the tiles put out by the company in their catalogues an invaluable aid to planning, and simply because of this small attention to detail the company won many customers. The company still survives as part of the H. & R. Johnson Richards Group which absorbed the majority of the old tile firms.

Minton Hollins and Co.

In spite of the tortuous legal battles over the use of the name Minton, Michael Daintry Hollins became the largest tile manufacturer in Victorian England, though by the turn of the century his position of supremacy was being seriously challenged by Maw & Co. Before Hollins took over complete control of the tile making side of the business at Minton & Co. in 1859, it was earning a respectable profit, but under his guidance the business grew rapidly and was no doubt the underlying cause for the friction between Hollins and his partner Campbell who ran the china works. When the partnership ended in 1868, Hollins built his new factory which covered over 7 acres (3 hectares) at Shelton Road, Stoke. By 1879 he was producing nearly 1½ million tiles a month,

ranging from simple mosaics to highly glazed art tiles. Twenty years later, with a workforce of over one thousand, output had risen to in excess of 2 million tiles a month.

Just before the partnership ended, however, Minton Hollins and Co. completed a major commission for the South Kensington Museum, where in addition to supplying over 40,000 square feet (3,700 square metres) of floor tiling, they supplied the tilework and faience for the Ceramic Gallery and the Refreshment Rooms. This scheme was the first of its kind to be undertaken on such a grand scale. Commissions such as these were instrumental in bringing in other similar work and in 1875 Minton Hollins and Co. were able to cite the following list of places for which they had supplied tiled pavements:

The Royal Palaces of Windsor, Osborne and Marlborough House; the Palace and State Yachts of the Sultan of Turkey; the Royal Residence of Prince Dhuleep Sing; the New Houses of Parliament, Westminster; the New Foreign Offices; the New Government Buildings in India; the South Kensington Museum; the New Albert Hall; the Senior and Junior Carlton Clubs; the Cathedrals of Ely, Lincoln, Litchfield, Gloucester, Wells, Glasgow, Armagh and Sydney (New South Wales); the New Capitol at Washington (U.S. of America); and many of the principal Ducal Mansions, Government Buildings, Churches and Public Institutions in Great Britain.

131. *Authors and Their Works*. Minton Hollins *c* 1880.
132. "Hamlet" from Minton Hollins' *Shakespeare* series *c* 1878.
133. *Religious Series*. Minton Hollins *c* 1875.

134. *Aesop's Fables*. Minton Hollins *c* 1875.

135. "Evening" from *The Times of Day*. Minton Hollins *c* 1880.

136. "Spring" from *The Seasons*. Minton Hollins *c* 1880.

137. *English History* by J. Moyr Smith. Minton Hollins *c* 1885.

138. One of a series of 10 nursery rhymes by J. Moyr Smith. Minton Hollins *c* 1880.

139. *Animals* by W. P. Simpson. Minton Hollins *c* 1885.

Though floor tiling played an important part in the company's trade, it also manufactured huge quantities of transfer-printed and majolica wall tiles. Its speciality was hand-painted tile panels of all sizes ranging from fireplace slabs to complete wall murals, and two artists in particular — Albert Slater and W. P. Simpson — aroused a great deal of interest. Albert Slater designed and painted four panels used at Longton Swimming Baths, Staffordshire, in 1886 which showed picture-book scenes of skating, bathing, ploughing and carting hay. Probably the largest contract in which the two men were involved was the tiling of a large butcher's shop in Belfast for which Simpson designed and painted two panels, both measuring 30 ft × 5 ft (9 m × 1.5 m) with about 750 tiles in each panel. The panels depicted sheep and cattle in a pastoral setting. Several other panels 10 ft high × 3 ft wide (3 m × 1 m) intended for the outside of the store were painted by Albert Slater which depicted antlered deer in a rocky landscape with groups of white ptarmigan sitting amongst the heather. He also painted several other panels for the game and fish departments in the rich, deep blues for which Minton Hollins was famous.

In common with its rivals, Minton Hollins also produced some transfer-printed picture tiles, though not in any great quantity. Gordon Forsyth was art director for two years from 1903 and obviously exerted a strong influence over much of the Art Nouveau tiling. In general though, established artists thought little of Minton Hollins' works. Writing in the *Art Journal* of 1895 Lewis

Day suggested that the factory had sacrificed art and design at the expense of perfecting mass-production technique.

Michael Daintry Hollins died in 1898. The factory survived the changing attitudes towards tiling through the 1920s and '30s, but finally closed in 1962 when it was absorbed into H. & R. Johnson Richards.

140. Panel by Albert Slater for Longton Swimming Baths 1886.

W. T. Copeland & Sons

141. "June" from *Months of the Year* by Lucien Besche. Copeland *c* 1875.

The firm of Copeland & Garrett in Stoke-on-Trent was one of the first to become seriously interested in the possibilities of tile manufacture and as early as 1837 it was making encaustic and other floor tiles. An interesting feature of these early tiles is that while the designs closely followed the medieval originals, no attempt was made to copy the traditional colours. They were not popular and so floor tile production was discontinued after only a few years. With the introduction of Prosser's patent, Copeland & Garrett revived its interest and began experimenting with the new technique. However most of its early designs are found on Minton Hollins' dust-pressed tiles. After 1847, when the partnership between William Taylor Copeland and Thomas Garrett was dissolved, dust-pressed tiles marked "Copeland" started to appear,

56

142. Design from a series of tropical birds *c* 1880.

143. Tile design from a Copeland pattern book giving precise decoration instructions *c* 1875-85.

144. Hand-painted on a Copeland tile with a similar surface to Minton China Works' patent Morocco finish *c* 1880.

145. Tile from *The Hunt*. Copeland *c* 1878.

146. Design from the *Robin Hood* series. Copeland *c* 1878.

147. Design from the *Shakespeare* series. Copeland *c* 1880.

148-149. Transfer-printed and hand-painted tiles showing the diversity of the Copeland designs *c* 1875.

57

150. Design from a Copeland pattern book for jug stands *c* 1895.
151. Painted by A. Bonffenier. Copeland *c* 1870.
152. *Months of the Year*. Hand-painted to Copeland designs on early Minton Hollins blanks *c* 1850.

but not in quantity, and it seems likely that the factory abandoned dust pressing in favour of high-quality plastic-clay tiles. Most of Copeland's plastic-clay tiles have a "combed" back which was made by drawing a blunted section of a coarse saw blade through the clay to provide a key for fixing. It has long been thought that Copeland was the only manufacturer to do this, but Burmantofts and Pilkingtons used the technique extensively on their plastic-clay tiles.

Copeland's reputation as an important tile manufacturer grew quickly. The company was unquestionably master of its craft. When the tenders were put out for the tiling of the new Imperial Library in Paris, designed by M. Henri Labrouste, every other tile manufacturer in Europe shrank away from the prospect of tiling nine cupolas with 4,000 painted slabs, all on the curve; in all, 36,000 tiles had to be curved across their length and breadth, with their radii decreasing towards the top of the cupola. In 1868 the library was opened with the cupolas faultlessly executed by W. T. Copeland & Sons.

Like all the leading tile manufacturers, Copeland had agents in

153. "The Painter" from Copeland's *Mediaeval Occupations c* 1877.
154. Design from the *Frog* series. Copeland *c* 1880.
155. Hand-painted on a Copeland blank by Shrigley & Hunt *c* 1880.

the principal cities and was well represented by travelling salesmen who carried with them hand-drawn sample books. Most of its competitors used printed catalogues, and it is characteristic of Copeland's close attention to detail and fine craftsmanship that its catalogues were hand painted.

Copeland tiles range from the simple geometric patterns of the 1840s and the miniature mosaics painted on a small printed grid, to the transfer-printed and hand-coloured medieval subjects. The majority of its hand-painted tiles can only be described as masterpieces of the ceramic art. Particularly fine are the simple overglaze decorated tiles, intended to complement Copeland's tableware, which were used as teapot or plant stands; and the whole tile schemes carried out for clients like Mr. MacFarlane, the eminent manufacturer of decorative ironwork. Copeland artists Lucien Besche, R. J. Abraham and Hurten painted panels for the billiard room of MacFarlane's new Glasgow house representative of health, strength, courage and fortitude. The latter panel included portraits of explorers Livingstone and Burton. Towards the end of the century, the company also produced a fascinating series of circular jug stands for Worthington, Bass, Allsopp's and other breweries.

Copeland discontinued tile production shortly after 1902.

Maw & Co.

When Samuel Wright's patent for the manufacture of inlaid tiles expired in 1844 it was bought in equal shares by Fleming St. John, his partner G. Barr of Worcester, and Herbert Minton. The Worcester company immediately began production of encaustic tiles. However, the local clays proved unsuitable and other materials had to be brought in from Shropshire. The business managed to struggle on for another four years before it finally closed. In 1850 George Maw and his brother Arthur bought up the ailing business and recommenced the manufacture of encaustic and other floor tiles; but faced with the same problems encountered by the old company, they moved, in 1852, to the Benthall Works at Broseley near Ironbridge, Shropshire, where the clays were better suited to tile making. The business did not assume a full manufacturing capability until 1857, though some encaustic

tiles were made before then, mostly derived from early medieval patterns. In 1856 Digby Wyatt began his long association with the company when he was commissioned to design a series of geometric mosaics.

By this time encaustic tiles were approaching the height of fashion. Maw & Co. began producing increasing quantities of two-colour encaustic tiles and tesserae for mosaics, and very quickly became a serious competitor to Herbert Minton. George Maw was one of the first to use six and more colours in encaustic tiles. He had an insatiable appetite for knowledge and travelled widely, visiting the mosques of the Middle East and the palaces of Europe where he made a careful study of the tilework on which he drew heavily when designing his own tiles.

Hand-prepared mosaics formed a large part of Maw's business in the 1860s and in order to bring a degree of mechanization to the laborious process a patent mosaic tile was first introduced in 1862 ". . . where the mosaic pattern is not obtained by assembling large numbers of polygons, but by incising their shape on a large panel, the incisions later being filled in with cement, the result being indistinguishable from a genuine mosaic except that each panel is identical." At the same time, George Maw was experimenting with majolica glazes and by 1871 he was in full-scale production of all kinds of majolica tiling. Faience followed, and by the 1880s Maw & Co. had become one of the most important and influential manufacturers of glazed architectural detail.

156. Unusual hand-painted, moulded tile. Maw & Co. c 1880.
157. 12 in × 6 in (30 cm × 15 cm) transfer-printed and hand-coloured tiles usually found 6 in × 6 in (15 cm × 15 cm) showing centre section only. Maw & Co.

158. Patent mosaic tile. Maw & Co. c 1885.

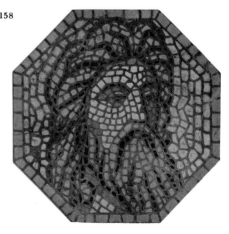

159. 2-tile panel from the *Japanese Series*. Maw & Co. *c* 1880.
160. Maw & Co. catalogue page illustrating designs by Walter Crane and others *c* 1880.

161. Majolica tile from *The Hanging of the Crane* series. Maw & Co. *c* 1875.

To help meet the steadily increasing demand for tiles from the home and the overseas markets, Maw & Co. installed the first ever steam-driven tile-making presses at the factory in 1873. This was just one of a series of mechanical improvements which ultimately led to the company moving its premises in 1883 to a more appropriate site at Jackfield in Ironbridge. Here production of tiles and faience continued at an unprecedented rate. At the height of the tile boom the company was producing over twenty million tiles and other items of faience a year. To help sell this phenomenal quantity of ceramic ware, the company used lavishly printed catalogues which showed the total range of their products — all nine thousand of them — the majority of which were available in

different colours to order. Maw even produced a special catalogue for colonial architects in which were listed a "few" persons and establishments to which its tiles had been supplied. The list ran to five large pages, and in addition to the Royal Family included Alexander II of Russia, two maharajahs, nine dukes, twelve earls, the railway companies, thirteen cathedrals, thirty-six hospitals, fifty-three public buildings, nineteen schools and colleges, and five warships. When it became a limited company in 1888, it boasted ten different kinds of decorated tiles in its catalogues from hand-painted and majolica relief tiles to gilt tiles in which the design was entirely executed in gold.

163-164. House swallow with a complementary floral basket. Maw & Co. *c* 1880.

165. A tile from the *Religious Series*.
Maw & Co. *c* 1875.
166. *Aesop's Fables* by C. O. Murray.
Maw & Co. *c* 1880.
167. "Navvy" from the *Trades* series.
Maw & Co. *c* 1880.

Transfer-printed and hand-painted picture tiles seem to have been in production from about 1874, and in common with the other tile companies, Maw used well-known free-lance designers to complement their own design staff, notably Walter Crane, Lewis Day and C. O. Murray. When C. H. Temple took up the position of senior resident designer in 1887 the free-lance designers were gradually displaced. Temple was a major force at the factory and besides designing a large number of tiles, he also perfected several new techniques; among them, a method of printing tiles from a photographically derived half-tone plate. In spite of its potential application, the process was never used to its fullest extent and lithographic printing remained the norm for many years to come.

The company entered the Art Nouveau era with a better chance of survival than most and emerged triumphant to go on into the 1920s and '30s, during which time it produced some unique geometrically inspired Art Deco tiles in slight relief, with an irridescent semi-matt glaze, which are much sought-after today.

In 1969, after many years successful use of silk-screen printing techniques, the company became part of the H. & R. Johnson Richards Group.

Craven Dunnill & Co.

When George Maw moved his factory to Jackfield he became neighbour to a company which was to become one of his major competitors. In fact to get to Maw's works one virtually had to pass the front door of Craven Dunnill & Co. whose factory was purpose built in 1871 on the site of an older tile works operated by Messrs. Hargreaves and Craven, once manufacturers of encaustic and other floor tiles. Even before Hargreaves and Craven set up business, there had been a tile-making pottery on the same site. The reason why Jackfield was so attractive to the tile makers was the abundant deposits of a rich red clay, the main constituent in encaustic tiles. Both Craven Dunnill and Maw had their own clay

168-173. A rare set illustrating the story of Cock Robin. Craven Dunnill c 1880.

workings there. Craven Dunnill & Co. rapidly gained a following using designs for encaustic floor tiles by such eminent architects as Alfred Waterhouse, George Goldie and John Bentley. Other architects, impressed by the quality of these tiles, chose to use them in the restoration of cathedrals and the building of new churches. Some of Craven Dunnill's pseudo-medieval floor tiles followed the originals so closely in design and method of glazing that they were difficult to tell apart. Like the other companies, it also manufactured a wide range of printed and enamelled tiles, specializing in majolica relief tiles. A subject on which it was particularly keen was that of diaphanously clad young ladies, decorated in majolica glazes using the *émaux ombrants* technique; in the same medium it also produced an interesting series of modelled portraits of prominent politicians such as Gladstone and Disraeli. The company's 1879 catalogue illustrates only a few picture tiles, but it is highly likely that at this time many of the anonymous picture tiles in circulation were in fact made by the company. In the main though, its tiles were unremarkable, with one or two notable exceptions: their ruby lustre tiles have always been sought after, and some fine unique stencilled work is also known to have been produced there.

The company managed to survive the ups and downs of the tile industry throughout the first half of this century and produced some very fine Art Deco friezes in the 1930s, but in 1951 Craven Dunnill closed its doors for the last time and thus ended eighty years trading from the Ironbridge Gorge.

174. Ruby lustre tile. Craven Dunnill c 1885.

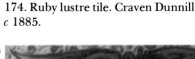

174

175

176

177

178

179

175. An extremely popular modelled majolica tile. Craven Dunnill *c* 1855.
176-177. "February" (left) and "August" from the *Old English* series by Wedgwood *c* 1878.
178-179. Modelled majolica tiles. Wedgwood *c* 1890.

180. Wedgwood patent impressed tile. A kind of mechanical barbotine process *c* 1880.

180

Josiah Wedgwood & Sons

Josiah Wedgwood's association with tiles began in 1761 when he sent some of his newly developed creamware to John Sadler of Liverpool for experimental transfer printing. By 1764 Sadler had overcome all the technical problems and was suitably organized to begin printing creamware, including tiles, on a large scale.

Wedgwood acquired his own printing facilities at Etruria, Staffordshire, and dispensed with the services of Sadler & Green. The Wedgwood creamware tiles quickly became popular and the firm seems to have been making a limited number of these plastic-clay tiles with the distinctive comb back right up until the introduction of Prosser's patent in 1840, and possibly until as late as 1867. An agreement made between Clement Wedgwood and the firms Toilet and Sanitaryware Makers refers to specific tile prices: "Tiles — Oak and Laurel wreaths. 2/6d per dozen, Vine wreaths . . . 2/6d per dozen, patent 6″ tiles 9d. and 8½″ tiles 1/- per dozen." Presumably the former were hand painted on plastic clay, and the patent tiles referred to were dust-pressed wall tiles. On the basis of this evidence it is clear that Wedgwood was producing dust-pressed tiles by 1867. But it was not until *c* 1870 that a proper tile department was opened where the firm manufactured the usual dust-pressed and plastic-clay encaustic tiles, tesserae for pave-

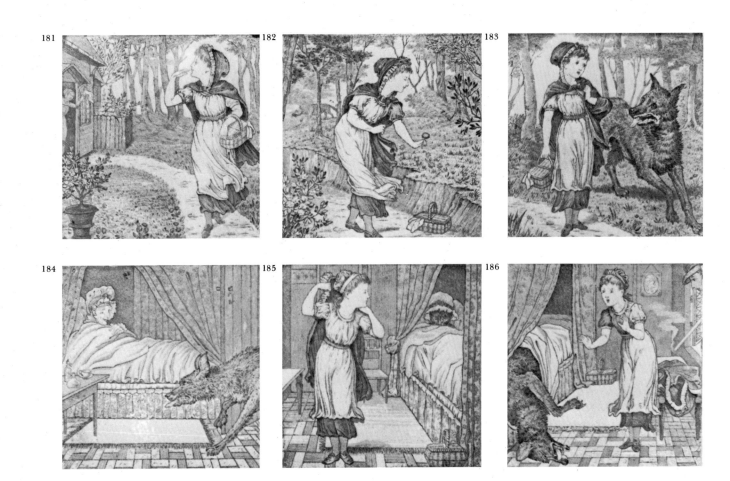

181-186. *Red Riding Hood* by Walter Crane (?). Wedgwood *c* 1878.

ments, and a limited number of majolica and transfer-printed wall tiles. By the middle of the decade, transfer-printed tiles began to play an increasingly important role. Large-scale production of transfer-printed tiles coincided with the arrival of Thomas Allen in 1876 and there can be no doubt that he was instrumental in directing the course of Wedgwood's tile production until he retired in 1906. Significantly, tile production also stopped about that time.

Many of the designs on the tiles were taken from tableware designs introduced at a much earlier date. For instance "Those Horrid Little Boys", one of a charming series of six tiles illustrating humorous encounters during the course of a day's fishing, appears on creamware dated 1871; and appears to have been introduced on tiles in 1878. The *Hats* series is a particularly good example of the use to which the factory put its designs. Though the central motif remained the same, the borders were varied extensively, each combination of design and border being identified by the use of a different pattern number. Further changes in pattern number were occasioned by the use of a different colour and thus it was possible to have one basic design in a wide range of differing colours and borders all identified by a different pattern number. Most conveniently, the majority of Wedgwood tiles have either the pattern number or the name of the series printed on the back. In common with other tile companies, Wedgwood had its own speciality: a patent impressed tile introduced to the factory by Mr.

66

187 and 189. *Musicians in an Orange Grove* by Walter Crane (?). Wedgwood *c* 1878.

188. Design from the *Infant Neptune* series. Wedgwood *c* 1878.

Marsden *c* 1880. It was made by a mechanical barbotine technique in which a coloured design was impressed in the tile body during manufacture, giving the finished tile a slight relief. Because of the purity of colour and the precision of line that could be achieved, the tiles were an instant success and won the company several medals. A major attraction of the process was that it could be applied to special designs without incurring extra costs.

The Wedgwood factory ceased production of tiles around 1902, though it still continued to decorate tiles made by T. & R. Boote and others right into the 1920s.

190. Tile from the *Dogs' Heads* series. Wedgwood *c* 1878.

191. Tile from the *Game* series. Wedgwood *c* 1878.

192-194. "Persian" tiles hand-decorated on plastic clay. Pilkingtons *c* 1900.

Pilkingtons Tile & Pottery Co.

Very few of the tile companies founded in the 1890s survived for more than a few years. The industry was already supporting many well-established manufacturers whose experience and foresight had consolidated their position as major producers. During the formative years of Art Nouveau, however, many businessmen were tempted to try their hand in the tile market, only to be swallowed up by the large companies or to go under. Pilkingtons Tile & Pottery Co. was probably the only newcomer to the industry at that time to survive intact. Success was achieved through a combination of manager William Burton's technical and artistic brilliance, craftsmanship second to none, and the expertise of a design team which included most of the eminent designers of the day: Walter Crane, C. F. A. Voysey, Lewis Day.

The factory was opened in 1892 at Clifton Junction, near Manchester, by the owners of the Clifton and Kersey Coal Company: the four Burton brothers. Test bores at a new mine shaft had revealed large quantities of marl (clay rich in carbonate of lime), a prerequisite for tile making. William Burton, at that time the chemist at Josiah Wedgwood, tested the clay and found it ideal for the manufacture of tiles. A year later, Burton left Wedgwood to start the new venture. On 13 January 1893 production of dust-pressed wall and floor tiles, and architectural faience began.

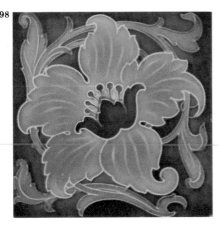

195, 197 and 198. Moulded tiles in rich majolica glazes pressed by machine to imitate tube-lined tiles. Pilkingtons *c* 1900.

PERSIAN · 800 · 1600 A·D·

196. A panel designed by Gordon Forsyth for the Liverpool Museum. Pilkingtons 1914.

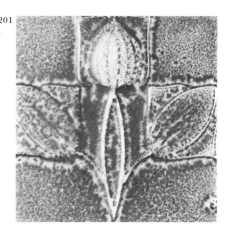

Although conditions were primitive — lighting consisted of candles stuck into clay, and heating was supplied by a fire in an old bucket — William Burton's enthusiasm and prowess in the chemistry of ceramics led Pilkingtons to a position of supremacy in the tile industry by the early twentieth century. His brother Joseph joined him as assistant manager and together they pioneered applied science and industry to ceramics.

The earliest tiles to come from the factory were plain white wall tiles and floor tiles in reds, browns and black. Before long, encaustic tiles were in production in a variety of colours and designs. Embossed and incised tiles followed the introduction of new tile presses, and by 1894 the business was in full production as manufacturer of all kinds of tiles. Block printing from steel plates came in 1895, and using the same presses, outline prints of floral designs were made and sent to the paintresses for hand colouring. A fireplace slabbing department was added and many new and colourful glazes were introduced. A pottery department was established in 1897, and by 1903 was producing the now famous Lancastrian ware. The pottery only accounted for about ten per cent of the business; tiles were still the main concern of the factory. However, spin-offs from the pottery greatly benefited the tiles and soon tiles were produced with the same glaze and lustre effects as on the pottery. By this time, at the height of the Art Nouveau era, the demand for tube-lined tiles was enormous, and new presses were installed to re-create the same effect.

199-200. Machine-pressed majolica tiles. Pilkingtons c 1900.
201. An "Egg shell" glazed tile — a spin-off from the production of Lancastrian ware. Pilkingtons c 1905.

The whole works was alive with excitement. Everyone from Burton down to the youngest apprentice was caught up in the feverish activity to develop new glazes, new techniques, new designs. It was in this atmosphere that the Pilkingtons designers found the inspiration to create some of the greatest examples of tile design the world has ever seen.

John Chambers, who later became chief designer, A. J. Kwiatkowski, and William S. Maycock were the first of the artists to arrive at the factory. Then came T. F. Evans, Lawrence Hall, E. Barratt and William Grinsdale. Between them they were responsible for all the decorated and modelled tiles produced at the works before 1900 and worked closely with the paintresses and other technicians at the factory. In 1899 Lewis F. Day was commissioned to design for the company, closely followed by Walter Crane, C. F. A. Voysey and J. Cassidy. Later still, came Gordon Forsyth (from Minton Hollins) as head of the artists, and though mainly involved in the new Lancastrian ware, he was the designer of some magnificent tilework; notably the panels in the Liverpool Museum (damaged by bombs in World War II) which he designed and painted. The five panels 18 ft × 9 ft (5.5 m × 3 m) depicted the great styles of historic pottery: Babylonian, Greek, Roman, Chinese and Persian. He also played a major part in the tiling of the ill-fated *Titanic*, in which Pilkingtons tiles were used extensively for the cabins and bathrooms.

A showroom was opened in Manchester, and representatives appointed throughout the rest of the country. An interesting facet of the representative's job was that once a year he would have to journey to Clifton Junction where he would meet with his colleagues to supervise the stock-take. By doing this, they acquired first-hand knowledge of the stock and could vary their sales pitch accordingly.

The Pilkingtons stand at the Glasgow Exhibition of 1901 displayed many unique designs and glaze effects for the first time, and was the first of many to promote Pilkingtons products to an admiring public throughout the world. The *Franco-British Exhibition Review* (1908) described the exhibition stands thus:

The most striking feature of the interior is a flattened Byzantine dome over the central part of the stand, which is encrusted with a mosaic of turquoise blue tiles relieved by narrow bands of silver lustre. The walls of the compartment on either side are decorated with painted tiles designed by Lewis F. Day and inspired by the beautiful tile decoration of Persia. The patterns are English enough in detail, but the colour schemes, of rich cobalt blue, sage green, bright turquoise and Rhodian red are similar to those used in the best Oriental work of the fifteenth and sixteenth centuries.

William Burton retired in 1915. Under his leadership the company had attained a position of prominence in a remarkably short time, and from which it was not to be dislodged. And even today, as part of the Thomas Tilling Group, the company remains an important manufacturer of glazed wall tiling.

71

Tile Manufacture in Poole

As a centre for tile production, Poole in Dorset was ideally situated. There were excellent clay beds, other raw materials could quite easily be brought in by boat and rail, and the finished tiles could be dispatched by the same means. John Ridgway, the well-known china manufacturer from Hanley, and his associates, T. R. and F. G. Sanders and T. S. Bull, seized the unique opportunity that Poole offered, and opened the Architectural Pottery Co. at Hamworthy in Poole, in 1854. The company's aim was to work directly with architects to fulfil their particular needs rather than to produce a speculative range of products. Most of its tiles were unremarkable, and its only real claim to fame was that William De Morgan used its tile blanks in fairly large numbers for his experimental work into lustre glazes. The chief technician at the Architectural Pottery was a Mr. T. W. Walker who left in 1860 to form his own company — T. W. Walker's Patent Encaustic & Mosaic Ornamental Brick and Tile Manufactory — in East Quay Road, Poole. Here he produced some colourful but ordinary work and very soon was in serious financial difficulties.

In 1873 Jesse Carter bought Walker's ailing East Quay Works and began to manufacture tiles. He had no more experience of the business than he had picked up as a partner in a builders' merchants. Accordingly, the first few years were a little difficult,

202. Gruesome encaustic roundel. Architectural Pottery Co. c 1860.
203. A geometric inlaid tile produced by T. W. Walker c 1865.
204. A tile by the Architectural Pottery Co. c 1870.

202

203

204

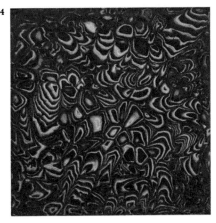

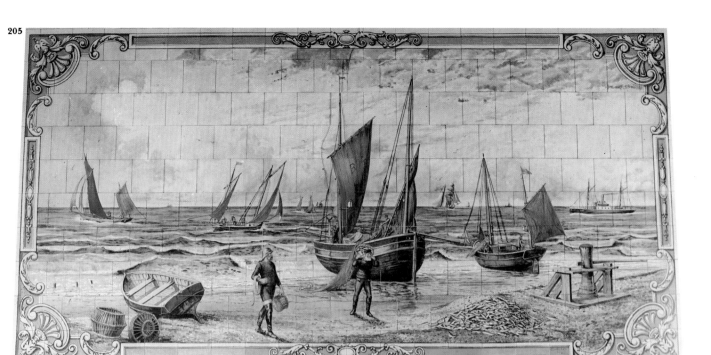

205. Hand-painted panel. Carter & Co.
c 1890.

but in 1881 the business was on a sound enough footing for him to take into partnership his sons Charles, Ernest and Owen. By 1883 the now world-famous Carter red floor tiles were being supplemented by glazed, modelled and painted tiles. Around this time the company began to produce its famous tile murals in public houses, hotels and large public buildings. The Rising Sun in Blackfriars, London, modernized in 1885, boasted a hand-painted panel entitled "Shakespeare and Ben Jonson in ye Olde Black-friars", in which Shakespeare and Ben Jonson were shown seated in conversation, waited upon by a fat, jovial landlord bearing a flagon and two glasses. Another Carter's panel in the Cambrian Distillery, Leicester Square, London, illustrated a famous local, seventeenth-century murder. In nearly all of Carter's tile panels can be found an historical association with the area in which they

206. Hand-painted tile panel by Carter
& Co. for a butcher's shop 1926.

were situated. A further attraction of Carter's panels for its clients  was that they tended to be far cheaper than those offered by its competitors. Practically all the panels are unsigned save for the name of the company.

Owen Carter became Art and Technical Director in 1893 and by 1895 the company was in a position to buy up the Architectural Pottery where it began to produce architectural faience and glazed ware, leaving production of plain floor tiles to the East Quay Works. Before Jesse Carter retired in 1901, the company bought a second works at Hamworthy which became known as the "White Works" when production began of the new white and cream tiles. Here Owen Carter, influenced by his friends William De Morgan and William Burton, started experimenting with tube lining, lustres and modelled majolica ware after the style of the Della  Robia plaques of the sixteenth and seventeenth centuries. These experiments culminated in the East Quay Works becoming the new artistic centre of the business in 1912. Henceforth all modelled, tube-lined, slip-painted, lustre, and other special tiles were made here, adjacent to the flourishing pottery business. World War I brought tile production to a standstill as building virtually ceased. A further blow to the company was the death of Owen Carter in 1919. To prevent a complete closedown, Charles Carter invited Harold Stabler and John Adams to form a subsidiary company and in 1921 Carter, Stabler & Adams was born. By now business was picking up and Carter & Co. began to exhibit new ranges of tiles and architectural faience. Outside designers were commissioned to complement the existing design team, but the majority of the design work was undertaken by John Adams and his wife, Truda. The decorated tiles they produced were popular right through to the 1940s even though they were produced at a time when the fashion was drifting away from decorated tiles towards a plainer, more subtle approach.

Major contracts were won for architectural and tiling work both at home and abroad, and once more Carter & Co. returned to a position of prominence within the industry. Its main speciality was swimming pools, but its regular clientele included chain stores, hotels, stations, restaurants and hospitals. Around 1925 Carter tiled the children's wards at the Middlesex Hospital with nursery rhyme and other children's panels designed by Haydn Jenson. London Transport commissioned Carter tile schemes for the underground railway stations. Carter was also involved in the tilework on the *Queen Elizabeth* and the *Queen Mary*. Reginald Till designed tube-lined schemes for the surrounding floor to the

207. Designed by Dora Batty for Carter & Co. *c* 1930.
208. Unattributed. Carter & Co. *c* 1930.

209. *Flowers (SH)* designed by Reginald Till for Carter & Co. *c* 1930.
210. From the *Farmyard* series by E. E. Stickland. Carter & Co. *c* 1930.
211. From the *Dogs* series by Cecil Aldin. Carter & Co. *c* 1930.

212. "Jack and Jill". Designed by Dora Batty for the *Nursery Rhymes* series. Carter & Co. *c* 1930.
213. From *The Chase* by Edward Bawden. Carter & Co. *c* 1930.

Queen Mary's swimming pool, and for the walls of the Turkish baths on the *Queen Elizabeth*. The particular advantage of tube-lined tiles as a swimming pool surround was that they offered an excellent non-slip surface.

Throughout the 1930s Carter was constantly improving its products and went on to follow the popular trends for slabbed fireplaces, and plain and mottled tiles. When decorated tiles started to come back into fashion, Carter pioneered the use of silk-screen decoration. In 1964 the company merged with Pilkingtons Tiles Ltd. and continues to produce a wide range of wall and floor tiles.

The Hereford Tile Manufactories

Tile production in Hereford began in 1851 when William Godwin set up his first factory at Lugwardine to manufacture bricks, quarry tiles and drain-pipes. He was joined in 1852 by his brother Henry who had been working for Maw at Worcester before the company moved to Ironbridge. Under Henry's guidance the two brothers began production of encaustic floor tiles. The business prospered, and the Godwins had to seek additional premises at which to manufacture bricks, while they retained tile production at Lugwardine. Their tiles were typical examples of the period — copies of the old English designs in reds and browns, inlaid with an ivory coloured pattern — and were used extensively in the restoration of medieval churches and cathedrals and in new buildings influenced by the Gothic revival.

In 1863 expansion was again necessary, and a new factory was opened at Withington. Here the brothers continued to manufacture a wide variety of encaustic tiles and tesserae using the new dust-pressing techniques alongside the traditional plastic-clay methods. Despite the popularity of Godwin's tiles, Henry left the company to form his own and in 1878 he opened the Victoria Tile Works. Here he produced a greatly expanded range of encaustic, majolica, enamelled, hand-painted and other tiles and soon overtook his brother to become the largest tile manufacturer in the area.

After Henry's departure, William Godwin went into partnership with his son and began trading as Godwin & Son. The factory still continued to operate as Godwin & Son long after William's death and even after it had been sold to Messrs. Lloyd & Puling in 1906. By the early twenties, the company was in trouble, and in 1927 H. & G. Thynne, which by this time owned the Victoria Tile Works, took on the business at Withington.

Four years after moving to the Victoria Tile Works, Henry Godwin went into partnership with William Hewitt, a former employee at Withington. Godwin & Hewitt continued to make a complete range of enamelled and encaustic tiles, including a patented fender which was made in one piece. A considerable

214

animosity arose between the rival Godwin companies over the years. In spite of the apparent prosperity of Godwin & Hewitt, it too became the victim of the decline in the tile industry and in 1909 became Godwin & Thynne, having been taken over by H. & G. Thynne who started to specialize in slabbed fireplaces and architectural faience. As many as five hundred fireplaces a week were being produced by 1921 when the new mottled tiles were in vogue. With the death of Henry Godwin in 1925, the firm finally became H. & G. Thynne. It acquired the Withington works and so united the two brothers' enterprises. Very few of Thynne's tiles were decorated, and those that were, were mostly decorated outside the firm. In 1957 Thynne's was bought out by Hereford Tiles, which continues to manufacture tiles on the old sites.

215

214-219. William De Morgan: 214, 216 and 217 are Early Fulham 1888-97; 215, 218 and 219 are Late Fulham 1898-1907.

William De Morgan

Artist, designer, potter, writer, William Frend De Morgan was a man of many talents whose influence over tile design and technique was felt throughout the whole industry. While studying at the Royal Academy, he fell under the influence of the Pre-Raphaelite painters and became drawn into the circle of artists and designers that was forming around William Morris. Shortly after meeting Morris, he abandoned his career in fine art and devoted himself to a life in the decorative arts. While working with Morris he designed stained glass and painted panels for use in the furniture designed by Morris, Webb and the others. From this

216

217

218

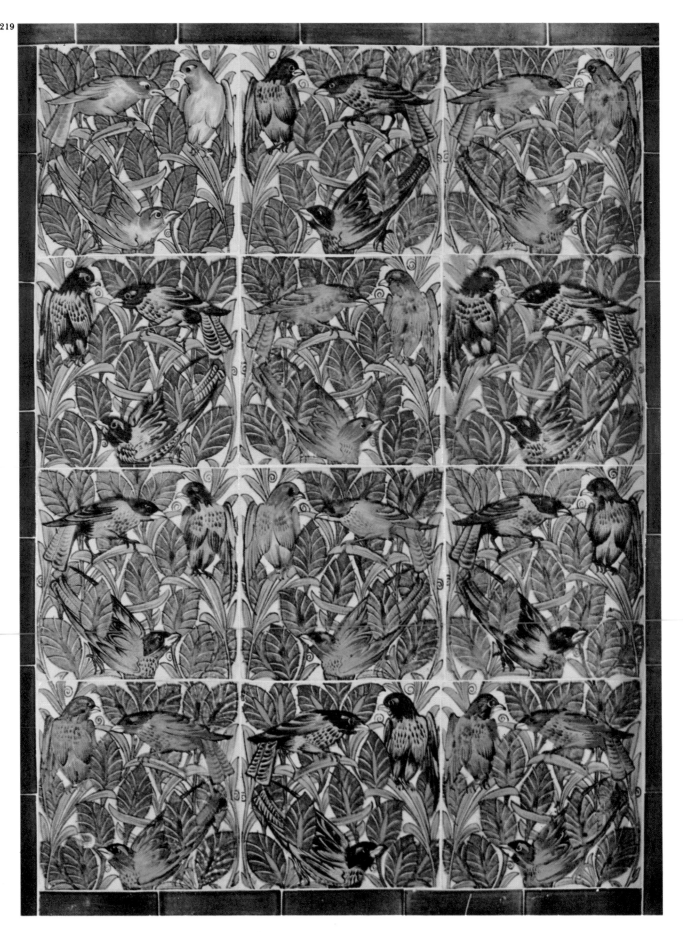

work an interest in tiles began to develop, and by 1869 he had set  up his own kiln at his lodgings in Fitzroy Square, London, where he began his experiments with lustre decoration on tiles. During the course of his work, his makeshift kiln arrangements caused the roof of the house to be burnt off and his landlord suggested that he find alternative premises. In 1871 De Morgan set himself up in Cheyne Row, Chelsea, with Frank Iles as his only assistant. By 1873 he needed larger premises which he was fortunate to find further down the street. From his new workshops he was able to increase his output of decorated tiles, which in the early years were painted on tile blanks from the Architectural Pottery Co., Carter, Wedgwood, and Craven Dunnill. During the "Chelsea Period", William De Morgan produced some three hundred tile designs, which provided many of his "standard" designs of later years. De  Morgan developed his own unique method for applying the design to the tile: a master drawing on translucent paper was pasted onto a sheet of glass, and on the other side, a clean piece of tissue paper was attached. Holding the "easel" against the light, the artist could easily copy the pattern onto the top sheet using a finished tile as a colour reference. The completed painting was then applied to a tile previously coated in a white slip to ensure the brilliancy of the colours, after which a powdered glaze was applied and the whole thing placed in the kiln and fired, during which time the paper burned away leaving behind the coloured pigments within the glaze.

As his techniques improved and the business grew, De Morgan began making his own biscuit from plastic clay, which greatly increased the cost of production, and ultimately, was one of the causes of his financial problems. However, it was on these tiles that De Morgan executed some of his finest work, including the Isnik tiles for Lord Leighton's Kensington house in 1877, where he completed the Islamic tiling scheme when it was found that there were insufficient original tiles to complete the job. De Morgan's tiles so closely matched the originals that it was almost impossible to differentiate between the two types.

Towards the end of his stay in Chelsea he was joined by Charles and Fred Passenger, who were to remain with him for over thirty years. The move to Merton Abbey, Surrey, in 1882 was influenced by expanding business and the fact that his friend William Morris had recently established his tapestry works there. At Merton Abbey tile production played only a minor role in the business as De Morgan became more involved with pottery. His marriage, worsening health and the new partnership with Halsey Ricardo prompted a return to London — to the new Sands End Pottery at Fulham, built by Ricardo in 1888.

By 1894 De Morgan's health had deteriorated to such an extent that he had taken to spending six months of the year in the more salubrious climate of Florence, but in the capable hands of the Passenger brothers and his partner Ricardo, who designed most of the relief tiles during this time, the business continued and won some significant contracts; the most important of which was the tiling of six of P. & O.'s luxury liners. Despite these encouraging

220-221. William De Morgan. Late Fulham 1898-1907.

222

223

222. Painted on Architectural Pottery Co. tile. William De Morgan *c* 1874.
223. Bath tiles designed by William De Morgan for Sir E. Debenham's London house 1906.

224. William De Morgan. Early Fulham 1888-1907.

224

commissions, De Morgan's absence was telling. The business went into a steady decline, culminating in the departure of Halsey Ricardo in 1898. A new partnership with the Passengers failed to set things right, and finally, in 1905, De Morgan was forced to retire through ill health; though the Passengers carried on for a further two years before closing the works in 1907. Remarkable man that he was, De Morgan was by no means finished, and at the age of sixty-seven he went on to become a well-respected and successful novelist.

There can be no doubt about De Morgan's influence on the mass producers of tiles. At its most apparent it can be seen in the Persian and lustre tiles made in the 1890s by such firms as J. C. Edwards, Maw & Co. and Mintons China Works; but it extends much further than that — into the basic concepts of design and the use of colour. De Morgan's approach was radically different from those of the other members of the Arts and Crafts Movement, who advocated a

79

return to medieval values and design. Certainly De Morgan drew on the past for his inspiration but he marked his work with his own unique interpretation.

Doulton & Co.

It was Henry Doulton's interest in the sanitary revolution that led to his firm's deepening involvement in architectural faience and tilework. From the 1820s he had been producing small architectural details for building work, alongside a staple range of drain-pipes and other waste-disposal products. By 1870 his company had enlarged its range to provide complete terracotta façades, the components being mass produced at Doulton's Lambeth factory; by 1891 Doulton & Co. was probably the largest

225

225. *Nursery Rhyme* panel designed by Margaret Thompson. Doulton *c* 1895.

manufacturer of sanitary ware and architectural terracotta in the world, with its additional works at Rowley Regis, near Dudley; St. Helens; Smethwick; Paisley; and Paris.

To meet the growing demand for a tile capable of withstanding the extremes of the English weather, Doultonware, a highly vitrified, salt-glazed stoneware, was introduced *c* 1876. Once the novelty had worn off, contemporary critics condemned the material as being too reflective. Doulton countered by developing Carraraware (*c* 1887), a semi-matt finished stoneware with the same durability as its predecessor. This material, with its wide range of decorative possibilities appeared to satisfy the pundits and became widely accepted.

W. J. Neatby, head of Doulton's architectural department from 1890 to 1907, perfected several new techniques while at Doulton, among them, Parian ware. This was an earthenware with a similar glaze to Carraraware which he used extensively on his tiled interiors. Other effects were created using terracottas, which were

226

226. Panel designed by William Rowe and painted by J. H. McLennan. Doulton *c* 1900.

painted and fired to produce a matt surface so that the overall effect was that of a fresco, hence the name vitreous fresco.

In addition to the architectural side of the business, Doulton also had a flourishing trade in hand-painted tile panels which were used in a multitude of buildings from schools to the underground railways. From about 1890 J. H. McLennan, John Eyre, Esther Lewis, William Rowe and Margaret Thompson designed and painted the vast majority of the firm's tile panels. William Rowe and Margaret Thompson are noted for the nursery-rhyme panels which were used in children's hospital wards all over the world. The company's reputation for tile panels was spurred on by the high esteem in which their individual tiles were held, some of which were printed and hand coloured, though most were hand decorated at the Lambeth Studio. Of these, probably the most well known are the incised stoneware tiles made by Hannah Barlow. Tiles were also painted at the Burslem Studio which Henry Doulton bought from Pinder, Bourne & Co. in 1882.

The extent to which Doulton was involved in the manufacture of dust-pressed tiles is a matter of some conjecture. The only impressed mark found on a Doulton dust-pressed tile is "Doultons Patent Safety Back"; all its other dust-pressed tiles can be identified as having being made by Webbs, Craven Dunnill and Mintons China Works. Bearing in mind that the firm was producing Doultonware, Carraraware and plastic-clay encaustic tiles, it seems likely that it was involved in dust pressing tiles, though on a limited scale. The company probably discontinued the process as being uneconomic. Both its hand-painted tiles and the cheaper printed versions were often used in conjunction with the other products made by the firm and were incorporated in "lavatories", bath surrounds, fireplaces and stoves.

The advent of World War I saw the end of Doulton's tile decorating activities. But the 1920s witnessed a return to ceramic decoration on building façades and Carraraware again became fashionable. Doulton finally closed its architectural department in 1956 and concentrated its activities on the production of tableware and other domestic products.

W. & E. Corn and the Henry Richards Tile Co.

In 1864 Edmund Corn, an established potter in Burslem, Staffordshire, took his sons, William and Edmund, into partnership. The company was called W. & E. Corn, and from its Navigation Road Works it made china and earthenware of all kinds. Not until 1891, shortly after a move to the Top Bridge Works in Longport, Staffordshire, and long after their father's death, did the two brothers start to produce glazed wall tiles.

227. Tube-lined panel by Doulton & Co. on Corn Bros. tiles *c* 1900.

Within a few years they had changed the name to Corn Brothers, and the factory began to establish itself as a major manufacturer of tiles. Its tiles at this time were typical of the period: transfer prints of flowered and geometric designs, some of which were hand tinted; panels for tile register stoves; and majolica tiles in several colours. Many of the designs were certainly "borrowed" from Mintons and others.

When the founders' grandsons took over the running of Corn Brothers, their freshness of ideas together with the arrival of Art Nouveau signalled a major change of approach in the company, and by 1900 it had a large share of the popular Art Nouveau tile market. Like its transfer-printed tiles, a great many of the firm's Art Nouveau tiles survive. In keeping with many of its competitors, Corn Brothers offered its tiles according to the colour requirements of its customers, and so it is quite common to see a popular design on a multitude of different-coloured tiles. In 1902 Alfred Henry Corn and Edmund Richards Corn moved to the Pinnox Works, hardly a stone's throw from Top Bridge Works, and began trading as the Henry Richards Tile Co., leaving Reginald Corn to look after the running of Corn Brothers until the factory closed in 1904.

The Henry Richards Tile Co. continued to flourish and produced a great many Art Nouveau designs, many of which it

228. Art Nouveau tiles from the Richards' catalogue *c* 1906.
229. Items from an H. Richards' catalogue page *c* 1900.

registered to give some degree of protection against unscrupulous "pirating". Production of floor tiles began in 1911 when a new factory was built adjoining the main Pinnox Works. To assure its independence, the company acquired the Burslem Mills Co. where it prepared its own raw materials. By 1931 the name of the firm was shortened to Richards Tiles.

In common with the other 1930s tile manufacturers, Richards made huge quantities of the new plain and mottled tiles in subdued colours, but retained its position in the market when others were in trouble. Eventually Richards merged with the Campbell Tile Co., and later with H. & R. Johnson.

Crystal Porcelain Tile Co.

The history of this firm is somewhat confused, but its products are among the most interesting from a technical point of view.

The story begins in the nineteenth century with the Crystal Porcelain Co. which was established at Cobridge near Stoke-on-Trent for the manufacture of industrial porcelain products. The company produced a very vitreous, extremely dense and completely non-absorbent tile. The tiles went straight from the artist — no glaze was applied — to the full heat of a Glost glazing kiln for twenty-four hours. During the firing the colour sank into the tile body and the finished tiles displayed a semi-gloss or polished finish. So confident was the company in the strength of these tiles it produced tiles a mere ⅛ in (3 mm) thick.

In 1881 the original company was taken over by the newly formed Crystal Porcelain Pottery Co., which continued to make the porcelain tiles and adapted the process to include giving the tiles a full glaze. It also began to introduce majolica and enamelled tiles. The name was changed in 1890 to the Crystal Porcelain Tile Co. when it stopped the manufacture of other porcelain products and concentrated on tiles. As well as the porcelain tiles, it produced a moderately successful range of encaustic and other decorative tiles, and mosaic pavements. Between 1896 and 1901 the company either closed or evolved into H. & R. Johnson, since by the latter date, H. & R. Johnson were trading at the same address.

230. Barbotine tile. Sherwin & Cotton *c* 1890.
231. "Niello" effect tiles from a Sherwin & Cotton catalogue page *c* 1890.

230

231

Sherwin & Cotton

Messrs. Sherwin & Cotton established their works in Vine Street, Hanley, Staffordshire, in 1877 and built a reputation for producing work of a consistently high quality. Their association with designer George Cartlidge is well known, and in addition to his "photographic" portrait tiles, he probably designed the large numbers of modelled majolica tiles that the company produced just before the turn of the century. The company also produced transfer-printed and other tiles — its floral barbotine tiles display an excellent understanding of the medium, and are some of the best examples of this kind of work. Sherwin & Cotton was also proud of its patented "Niello" effect which was "a revival of the old Italian method brought to perfection in the fifteenth century by Masodi Fininguerra's exquisite workmanship in gold and silver". The overall effect was one of a soft hand-painted tile. The

85

company also patented the "Lock Back" by which a tile could be affixed more securely to walls and roofs.

Sherwin & Cotton closed in 1911 when George Cartlidge took over the premises for his new venture.

J. C. Edwards

J. C. Edwards is reputed to have entered the ceramic manufacture business as a complete novice. By 1896 he was employing one thousand men and had an output of two million articles a month. However, decorated tiles formed only a very small percentage of this figure. The encaustic, majolica and embossed tiles are fairly representative of their period, but Edwards's real claim to fame lay in the ruby lustre and other tiles designed for him by L. A. Shuffrey in imitation of De Morgan's work.

When Edwards died in 1896, the running of the business was taken on by his two sons, and it finally ceased trading in 1958.

T. & R. Boote

Thomas and Richard Boote moved to the Waterloo Works, Burslem, Staffordshire, in 1850, where they manufactured encaustic tiles by the plastic-clay method. In 1863 they joined Messrs. Boulton and Worthington in patenting a method for dust pressing encaustic tiles which brought the price of encaustic tiles within the reach of the ordinary householder for the first time.

By the late 1870s T. & R. Boote was manufacturing transfer-printed and majolica tiles. A very popular set of transfer-printed tiles was designed for the company by Kate Greenaway in 1881 depicting the four seasons with children dressed in typical Greenaway style. At the turn of the century, T. & R. Boote was probably responsible for more majolica tiles than any other manufacturer, producing a great many popular Art Nouveau designs; and between 1892 and 1897 upwards of half a million plain white Boote's tiles were used in the construction of the Blackwall Tunnel under the Thames in London. This figure probably represented only two or three months' output of this kind of tile from Boote's works.

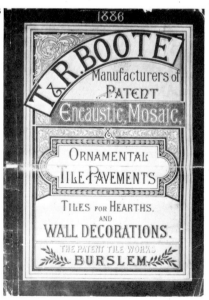

George Wooliscroft & Sons

George Wooliscroft started in business at a brick yard in Chesterton, Staffordshire, in 1849. He produced bricks and quarry tiles and in a few years began to make encaustic floor tiles. Additional works were acquired at Etruria and Hanley, and by 1900 the range of tiles available from George Wooliscroft & Sons was

232. A mixture of Japanese and Aesthetic influence. Unattributed. Probably produced by T. & R. Boote *c* 1875.
233. Title page of T. & R. Boote's 1886 catalogue.

certainly equal to, if not better than, that from many other companies. Its products included hand-painted art tiles; lustred, enamelled, barbotine and majolica tiles; encaustic, tessellated, quarry and roofing tiles; a special floor tile produced by a hydraulic press; ironstone adamant tiles; and chromoglaze printed tiles. In addition to these there was the company's speciality: plain-coloured fresco tiles. Wooliscroft's Moorish mosaic was extremely well thought of and looked most effective when set off in large panels. Another unusual product was the "Anglo-Dutch" tile — hand painted to order from a client's photograph or print.

George Wooliscroft & Sons is one of the few Victorian tile firms to stand the test of time, and it still manufactures high-quality tiles for floors and external cladding.

234. An unusual tile for H. A. Ollivant who tended to concentrate on majolica and transfer-printed floral designs.

Henry Abraham Ollivant

Ollivant began trading from the Etruscan Tile Works, Cliff Vale, Stoke-on-Trent, in the 1890s, probably only decorating tiles for the first few years. By 1895 he was manufacturing an extensive range of transfer-printed, hand-painted and majolica Art Nouveau tiles. In the early part of this century, he was a regular client of the Design Registration Office, though many of his designs are similar, if not identical, to some of Maw's Art Nouveau designs. After 1908 he faded into obscurity, like so many other tile entrepreneurs of the period.

Malkin Edge & Co.

In 1866 James Malkin and Joseph Edge decided to expand their already well-established business and enter the new lucrative tile market. They opened the Patent Encaustic Tile Works at the Newport Pottery, Burslem, where they manufactured dust-pressed tiles of every description with an eye to the popular market. Their speciality was slabbed hearths and fireplaces on which they used plain, embossed, incised and hand-painted majolica tiles. A feature which seemed to be uniquely theirs was a hearth with a "beautifully finished landscape" surrounded by sympathetically coloured geometric tiles, supplied with matching grate panels. Though the firm was not prolific in its output of picture tiles, some examples are known, the best of which are a series of twelve "games" played by characters in medieval dress.

After the death of Joseph Edge, the firm changed its name to the Malkin Tile Works Co. Ltd. and became one of the few companies to survive the transition into the twentieth century unscathed. In addition to producing the mottled tiles of the twenties and thirties it was able to produce a limited number of decorated tiles following the trend set by Carter & Co. of Poole. In 1968 the company joined with H. & R. Johnson Richards.

235

W. B. Simpson & Sons

W. B. Simpson and Sons are one of the best known of the art tile decorators working in the 1870s and '80s.

In a move to break away from the convention of mass-produced tiles, independent decorators set themselves up to provide a service to their more discerning clients. An old-established firm of painters and decorators, Simpson, also the London agents for Maw, began decorating tiles and glass around 1870, and in 1871 its reputation for this kind of work was further enhanced when it displayed a magnificent chimney-piece at the Kensington Exhibition.

Unlike many of its competitors Simpson preferred to paint directly onto tile biscuit and glazed the tiles directly on the premises. The brilliancy and purity of colour it achieved by this method far surpassed anything produced by other tile decorators who were simply painting overglaze. Simpson was justifiably proud of its work, and boasted that all its products were executed by its own highly skilled staff of artists and craftsmen. It did, however, use designers from outside the company, notably A. Waterhouse who designed the tiles for Eaton Hall in 1877 for the Duke of Westminster, and H. Walter Lonsdale who was responsible for the set of twelve tile panels depicting scenes from the Book of Kings which were installed in the Bute Tower in Cardiff Castle in 1876.

The company was also well known for its individual tiles, fireplaces and mosaics. An excellent example of the latter was laid at the Fitzwilliam Museum, Cambridge, where the pavement was constructed of ½ in (13 mm) ceramic cubes. Despite the obvious difficulties involved in this type of work, the floor was considered to be much harder wearing than marble. It was certainly much cheaper and absolutely damp proof.

W. B. Simpson & Sons faded into obscurity before the turn of the century.

236. Hand-painted tile. W. B. Simpson & Sons *c* 1885.

236

CHAPTER FOUR

Design
and Designers

The first recorded use of the word "decorative" when applied to industrial production dates to about 1791 when the Industrial Revolution was approaching its height and was transforming the fundamental thinking behind the traditional handmade crafts. Decoration of some kind was soon extended to cover the whole spectrum of mechanically produced wares from cast iron to pottery, and came to be thought of as a desirable artistic flourish that could be applied to almost any surface. In this context the whole design process was succinctly described as applied art. It soon became apparent that applied art was changing from a desirable element to an absolute necessity if the manufacturers were to continue to sell their wares and maintain economic production. In the forty years after 1843, well over 400,000 designs were registered at the Patent Office covering everything from lace and textiles, to gate posts, coffee-pots and even the whalebone in ladies' corsets.

Basic design concepts stretch back into antiquity and though a design may be modified, updated to cater for modern taste or adapted for a particular method of production, the fundamental elements within the design remain constant. A design can exist without colour, but with its addition, further elements are created which complement the original design concept. The early Victorians looked to past design for their inspiration, but did little to update it, and so we find examples of Roman, Greek, Renaissance and medieval ornamentation, followed later, as fashions changed, by Egyptian, Persian and Japanese designs. With an increasing awareness of design and its applications, both in the manufacturing process and in the final usage of the decorated object, there came a gradual shift away from copying towards innovation.

In the 1830s, around the time that Herbert Minton was experimenting with encaustic tiles, design was generally at a low ebb; industrial production was far more important than good design. Nevertheless the Victorian fervour for the building and restoration of churches was rapidly gaining impetus and England was on the threshold of the Gothic revival, led by Augustus Pugin. Working closely with Herbert Minton, he designed a great many pseudo-medieval tiles for churches, schools and country houses, and between them they were responsible for establishing the encaustic tile as an integral part of English floor design. Other architects followed suit and began designing tiles which they had made for them by Minton, Copeland & Garrett, and others. As the manufacturers became more confident, new designs were introduced and the factories began to employ their own design staff. By 1860 the two-colour medieval reproductions had been superceded by tiles, inlaid with up to five colours, which owed little to medieval influence.

The introduction of Prosser's patent opened up new horizons and Pugin was quick to take advantage. As before, others followed; but what was good for the floor was not necessarily good for the wall and there was a real need for a new style of decoration to keep pace with improvements in industrial technology and mass production. Collins and Reynolds' patent for printing tiles was introduced but it was a technique, not a decorative style. The real problem lay in the dichotomy between Art and Industry which was admirably highlighted in the Great Exhibition of 1851, where the main criticism was levelled at the poor aesthetic quality of the otherwise technically excellent manufactured goods. However, help was at hand and already a group had been formed which was actively opposed to the industrialization of design and mass production. Through their painstaking methods of working, their meticulous attention to detail and their sympathy with medieval design, the Pre-Raphaelite artists were the first to draw attention to the importance of design and colour in everyday life. The work of Rossetti, Millais, Hunt and later Madox Brown, Burne-Jones and William Morris contained deep moral undertones conveyed through a return to romanticism and medieval art. When allied to the teachings of John Ruskin, who also urged a return to medieval standards and values of craftsmanship, their influence was considerable. Some tile manufacturers took note of the undercurrents that were forming around them, but while they sympathized with Ruskin and his contemporaries they were in the business of mass producing tiles that were acceptable to the majority, not of manufacturing beautifully finished, handmade articles which ultimately could only be available to a few. Still, there was room for compromise, but it took another twenty years before the two opposing points of view were reconciled.

In the meantime, Morris set up Morris, Marshall Faulkner & Co. in 1861. His first direct dealings with tiles came in 1862 when he wanted to use them in the fireplace at his Red House. As he was under the impression that all English tiles were machine made, he imported handmade tiles from Holland. From then on the company had occasional dealings with tiles but they did not form a major part of its output; rather its designs proved to be a source of inspiration to other tile manufacturers who were waking up to the idea that something was happening in design. Morris and Co., as it later became in 1865, firmly established itself as the cornerstone of the Arts and Crafts Movement.

A contemporary of Morris, William De Morgan, shared his belief in the unity that was possible through a combination of craft and design, and produced some of the finest examples of tilework that

90

237-238. Designed by Christopher Dresser for Mintons China Works c 1875.

had yet been seen. His exceptional artistic talent and his enthusiastic, innovative approach to ceramics enabled him to achieve what so many of the industrial art potters failed to do. His tiles and pottery were unique, not only in the design sense, but in the colours and in the effects he managed to create. Like Morris, his designs were widely imitated, particularly his lustre ware. The technique of working with lustres was already well known to the Staffordshire potters and yet they failed to apply it to tiles because it was not fashionable. It took somebody like De Morgan to waken the industry to the potential. His Persian wares, which drew on the much earlier Isnik designs, were also widely copied. The tile manufacturers and designers knew of this style of decoration long before De Morgan yet had not been prepared to commit themselves until the style became popular.

By the 1870s and '80s, however, certain manufacturers were beginning to take the initiative, perhaps reassured by the success of the Arts and Crafts workers. Those that did not very soon went out of business. Mintons' Art Pottery Studio which was set up in 1871 is an excellent example of how one company rose to meet the challenge, and very soon it was producing wares that rivalled, and in some cases bettered, the finest of the craft revivalists.

In 1875 Liberty & Co. opened a shop in London where it specialized in all things oriental. The shop attracted Gabriel Rossetti, Burne-Jones, E. W. Godwin and most of the free-thinking designers and played a vital role in the acceptance of oriental art as a major design influence. The Japanese influence was further reinforced by Christopher Dresser who had visited Japan in 1877.

These were the formative years for what came to be known as the Aesthetic Movement, which attempted to bridge the gap between ordinary people and the exclusive followers of the Arts and Crafts Movement. Popular book-illustrators Walter Crane and Kate Greenaway were commissioned to design tiles that would be mass produced. Stacey Marks and Moyr Smith for Mintons, Thomas Allen of Wedgwood, and many other painters and designers produced designs that drew on Arts and Crafts influence. It was the decoration that was popular, not the technique. The majority of people could not have cared less how the tile was made, they liked the design, and they bought it.

Still the Arts and Crafts Movement flourished and as it created new approaches to design, so the industrialists drew on its inspiration to cater for an ever increasing public demand. But the dream of handmade perfection, commendable as it was, could not survive the pressures of business and the craft potters suffered in the face of stiff competition from the large manufacturers. Their tiles had to be expensive because of their extremely limited manufacturing facilities. When De Morgan began trading he had one assistant and worked from an old house in Chelsea, and even at the height of his career, the total factory personnel could be counted in tens. A large commercial manufacturer sometimes employed over a thousand people.

Despite their apparent popularity, not all the Arts and Crafts workers found favour with the public; there were those that doubted their motives. If they were so concerned about regenerating a spirit of craftsmanship among working people, why were their products so expensive that only the wealthy could afford them? To the uneducated eye their tiles were far from perfect; and for the price of one, twenty perfect machine-made tiles could be bought. By the turn of the century, the craft revivalists had resigned themselves to machine production, but at least in part they had achieved their objectives by restoring the basic concepts of integrity and craftsmanship to industrial production. The artists and designers thrown up by the revival were too vigorous to rest content, and from their restlessness was born Art Nouveau with its

239. Hand-painted tile signed by one of two Japanese artists employed at Mintons China Works *c* 1880.
240. Majolica tile. Maw & Co. *c* 1880.
241. Aesthetic-influenced tile. Mintons China Works *c* 1880.

all-embracing, sensuous, sweeping lines and imaginative use of colour. Lewis Day, C. F. A. Voysey and Walter Crane pioneered the New Art on tiles, working with Maw and Pilkingtons. Other companies followed suit and during the twenty years up until 1910 some tile manufacturers turned virtually their whole production over to the new art form. New companies sprang up, content to ride the crest of the wave and to retire when it was over. Towards the end of World War I, the seeds of Art Deco were being planted, and by 1920 the new Decorative Art had arrived based on angular and geometric principles. But as the social conditions changed, so did the fashion in domestic interiors. Tiles in plain pastel shades became popular, particularly for slabbed fireplaces and bathrooms. Some firms continued to produce decorative tiles: Carter and Pilkingtons commissioned well-known designers in the 1930s, but they too eventually succumbed to the trend for subdued patterns and colours.

Practical Design Considerations

Probably the most common single mistake in tile design was a complete lack of appreciation of the power contained in a repeated pattern. Many designers failed to grasp that the six-inch-square design on which they were working would not be used in isolation — that it would be used as part of an overall scheme — and that while their single tile might be technically and artistically perfect, when it was used in conjunction with other similar tiles, the result could be an absolute disaster. Even as late as 1910, when Art Nouveau majolica relief tiles were at their most popular, very few of them were suitable for use in repeated patterns. Individually they were beautiful, together the effect was overwhelming.

The use of colour was another major stumbling block, and a failure to grasp the fundamentals of light and colour led many designers astray. As Halsey Ricardo said "the glory of a tile is its colour . . . the pattern is little more than a set of pegs on which to hang the colours." Sometimes it seemed as if the designers were

93

totally devoid of colour sense and the most peculiar combinations  of colour appeared which completely ruined any merit the original design may have had.

Designers' appreciation of tile usage was generally better. They very quickly found out that majolica relief tiles were not the ideal flooring material and that heavy encaustic tiles were not suited to wall decoration. Tiles intended for use in a fireplace, for instance, had to conform to certain obvious design criteria. Similarly, tiles for external use had their own design restraints. They had to be frostproof and able to withstand severe weather without adverse effects, and the designs had to be bold and relatively simple so they could be seen from a distance.

Of course, not all the blame for bad tiling can be apportioned to its creators. Customers were just as likely to be at fault through their basic ignorance of the medium. They may have used tiles together that should never have been used in that way, or used the wrong tiles for the wrong job. In these instances the designers had probably done their best; if the customers insisted on things being done the wrong way then that was their business.

244. "Cobweb" from the *Midsummer Night's Dream* series by Thomas Allen. Wedgwood *c* 1878.

Designers

It would be impossible to compile a list of all the personalities who were directly involved with tile design or who influenced the theory behind the designs. Social commentators like Ruskin exerted a profound influence over both the designers and the public but he was never directly responsible for designing tiles, nor was he a particularly powerful advocate of their use. Other influential artists and designers were instrumental in directing the course of design, but again they were not directly involved in designing tiles. The following list comprises designers and others who were instrumental in the rise of the Victorian tile, though it must be remembered that tiles generally took up only a small part of their time.

Robert Frederic Abraham (1827-95)

In 1865 R. F. Abraham succeeded George Eyre as art director at W. T. Copeland & Sons, where he remained until he died in 1895. It is most probable that he was responsible for some of Copeland's most magnificent tile designs. Prior to working at Copeland he had been involved in the decoration of porcelain at Coalport and had been the art director at Hill Pottery, Burslem.

Robert John Abraham (1850-1925)

R. J. Abraham worked at Copeland under the art directorship of his father and from about 1875 was one of its major tile designers. In addition to working on a wide range of transfer-printed tiles, he was also well known for his ability as a tile painter, particularly of

245-247. 3 tiles from the *Hats* series by Thomas Allen. Wedgwood *c* 1880.

248. A design by Thomas Allen for the *Courses of a Meal* series. Wedgwood *c* 1878.
249. "Rebecca repelling the Templar" by Thomas Allen from the *Ivanhoe* series. Wedgwood *c* 1880.

portraits. He designed and painted a tile frieze commissioned by Mr. MacFarlane of Glasgow which chronicled the sporting ages of a British gentleman.

Thomas Allen (1831-1915)

While working for Mintons (*c* 1845) Thomas Allen was attending classes at Stoke-on-Trent School of Art, from where he won a scholarship which took him to the School of Design in London. In 1854 he returned to Mintons where he specialized in painting figures and flower subjects after the fashionable Sèvres style of decoration. He also designed and painted tiles and though none of his designs are signed it is fairly safe to assume that he was responsible for one of the series of Aesop's fables, since in many respects they are identical to some of his work at Josiah Wedgwood & Sons after he moved there in 1875. Wedgwood's move into picture tiles more or less coincided with Allen's arrival there. Series which can definitely be attributed to Thomas Allen are *Midsummer Night's Dream*, *Ivanhoe*, *Courses of a Meal* and *Hats*, though he was probably responsible for a great many more. In 1880 he became art director, a position he held until his retirement in 1900.

Joseph François Leon Arnoux (1816-1902)

Leon Arnoux became art director at Mintons in 1849 after several years working as a designer for the company. As art director he was responsible for many major innovations, both technical and artistic, and though he personally may not have designed tiles, his achievements with enamels and majolica glazes opened up new and exciting possibilities for the whole tile industry.

Hannah Barlow (1851-1916)

In 1871 Hannah Barlow became one of the first female artists to work at Doulton's Lambeth Studio. Her characteristic incised studies of animals and country scenes are mostly restricted to salt-glazed earthenware but examples of her tiles are known.

Lucien Besche (d. 1901)

French-born porcelain painter Lucien Besche worked at Mintons for a short time before joining Copeland in 1872. He mainly worked on porcelain-ware figure subjects, but he also designed and painted tiles while at Copeland. Those depicting the twelve months of the year in blue and in polychrome are among his best known. He left Copeland in 1885.

Antonin Boullemier (1840-1900)

Although usually associated with Mintons, where he worked for twenty-eight years prior to his death, Boullemier also painted tiles for Copeland. He specialized in idyllic figure studies and putti, executed mostly on earthenware and porcelain; though his designs were also applied to tile panels.

Ford Madox Brown (1821-93)

One of the Pre-Raphaelite school of painters, Madox Brown became a founder member of Morris, Marshall, Faulkner & Co. in 1861, where he painted, designed stained glass and furniture, illustrated books, and made the occasional foray into textile and tile design. Together with D. G. Rossetti he produced a series of tiles in 1863 which portrayed seasonal occupations and which were used at Queens' College, Cambridge.

William Burgess (1827-81)

William Burgess began his career as an engineer, but in 1840 he joined the offices of Digby Wyatt where he designed several cathedrals and a great many churches. Most of the tiles used in them were of his own design and made by Maw & Co. He was an exponent of the medieval approach to craftsmanship

Edward Burne-Jones (1833-98)

Burne-Jones exerted a powerful influence on all aspects of Victorian decorative art. As a designer, he was closely linked with the Pre-Raphaelites and later, the Aesthetes. His fascination for medievalism, coupled with his dislike of modern industrial society, featured strongly in his work. William Morris and Burne-Jones became firm friends while attending Exeter College, Oxford, and both were deeply influenced by the work of Rossetti, Hunt and Millais. Under Rossetti's guidance, Burne-Jones left the college without graduating and shared lodgings with Morris in Red Lion Square, London. As a founder member of Morris, Marshall, Faulkner & Co. he designed stained glass, tapestries, decoration for pianos and organs, gesso work and tiles. He was the originator of most of the decorative tiles and panels made by Morris & Co.

John Henry Chamberlain (1831-83)

As an architect Chamberlain came strongly under Ruskin's influence and firmly believed in the Gothic approach, particularly

250

250. Morris & Co. panel by Burne-Jones *c* 1872.

251. Morris & Co. tile possibly designed by Burne-Jones.

with regard to public buildings, in which he saw a need to improve visual contrasts. To this end he produced his own tile designs which were executed by Maw & Co.

William Steven Coleman (1829-1904)

After training as a naturalist Coleman went on to work for W. T. Copeland. In 1869 he began designing for Mintons in a free-lance capacity and in 1871 became director of its Art Pottery Studio in Kensington. He specialized in japan and classical English subjects, and is renowned for his studies of naked children and cherubs. As a painter he moved away from wholly underglaze decoration, preferring to work overglaze in bright enamels, sometimes using an underglaze brown outline as the basis of the design. Many of his designs were painted by other artists at Mintons both in Stoke and at Kensington, and his influence can be felt on many of the company's tiles, particularly those of William Wise.

Walter Crane (1845-1915)

The name of Walter Crane is synonymous with Victorian book-illustration but in fact this aspect of his career was only one of many. After completing an apprenticeship in wood engraving during which time he was also studying painting, he began to make his name as a book illustrator. His first book *The New Forest, Its History and Scenery*, written by J. R. Wise, was published in 1836. Crane's future as a book illustrator was secured with the publication of *The Baby's Opera* (1877) and *The Baby's Bouquet* (1878). His first connection with Wedgwood seems to date from about 1867 and lasted for about ten years, though examples of Wedgwood pottery decorated some years later by Crane are known. That he designed tiles for them is not certain, but on the available evidence is highly likely. The *Little Red Riding Hood* series, though unsigned, bears all the hallmarks of Crane's work. And a further series of Renaissance-influenced musicians in an orange grove features figures that are practically identical to those in *The Baby's Own Aesop* illustrated by Crane in 1886. Many of Crane's tile designs pre-date their appearance in books, and this is certainly true of the Wedgwood *Musicians* series.

252-254. Hand-painted and underglazed. Mintons China Works to designs by Walter Crane c 1880. Signed A. P.

During the 1870s Crane also worked at Mintons China Works. Hand-painted tiles of illustrations from the *Baby's Bouquet* and the *Baby's Opera* are occasionally found on Mintons' tiles. These could have been painted elsewhere but Crane's presence at the works weighs heavily against this possibility.

By far the greatest proportion of Crane's tile designs were undertaken for Maw & Co. in the 1870s and '80s, for which he produced a great many transfer-printed and moulded tiles including *The Seasons*, *The Times of the Day* and a panel entitled "Ploughing". There can be no doubt about the authenticity of these designs since most of them bear Crane's familiar rebus. In 1880 Crane became art superintendent of the London Decorating Co., a firm specializing in encaustic tiles; its success seems to have been limited since few references to it remain. Crane's involvement was probably only that of consultant.

Walter Crane also designed for Pilkingtons around the turn of the century, where in addition to producing a set of one-piece tile panels portraying the senses, he also experimented with the popular tube-line technique and many of his designs were adapted for press moulding. His skill as a designer was more than matched by his acumen in business and he was never slow to capitalize on the popularity of his designs.

As founder member of the Art Workers Guild, president of the Arts and Crafts Exhibition Society and later principal of the Royal College of Art in 1898, Crane's teachings on the application of art and his books on the theory of design exerted a powerful influence on contemporary design thinking.

255. Design by Walter Crane *c* 1885. Produced by Steele & Wood.
256. Lustre tile designed by Lewis Day for Maw & Co. *c* 1880.
257. William De Morgan. Merton Abbey 1882-8.

258. William De Morgan. Early Fulham 1888-97.
259. Triple lustre tile. William De Morgan. Merton Abbey 1882-8.

Lewis Foreman Day (1845-1910)

Lewis Day was a prolific designer and an important influence in the Arts and Crafts Movement. In addition to lecturing and writing on the subject of design he was a founder member of the Art Workers Guild and of the Arts and Crafts Exhibition Society. He started work as a clerk in the firm of Lavers and Barraud, specialists in glass painting, and later moved on to become a stained-glass designer with Clayton & Bell. By 1870 he had started his own business concentrating on the design of interior furnishings, textiles, stained glass, wallpapers and tiles. Unlike Morris, Day conceded that the machine, properly harnessed, could be an asset to the craftsman. He also believed that the craftsman was just as important as the designer. As the first of a new breed of professional designers, Day exerted considerable influence on the tile industry.

His *fin de siècle* tile designs for Maw, Pilkingtons and J. C. Edwards, which all have a strong emphasis on line, are typical of his well-proportioned, naturalistic approach to design.

William Frend De Morgan (1839-1917)

De Morgan was one of the most influential and innovative tile designers of the late nineteenth century. His admiration for the Pre-Raphaelite painters led to a close friendship with William

Morris. De Morgan's design techniques and business interests are discussed in the preceding chapter.

Christopher Dresser (1834-1904)

Christopher Dresser, probably the earliest, and certainly one of the most successful, of the independent mid-Victorian designers, started his career as a botanist. However, he managed to maintain an active interest in design, kindled in youth during two years' study at the School of Design in London, and in the 1860s he began to design pottery. Many of his designs for Mintons were produced at the Art Pottery Studio in Kensington, and though very few tile designs can be directly attributed to Dresser, his influence was felt right across the industry. It was he who was largely instrumental in popularizing Japanese-influenced decoration on tiles.

George Eyre (1818-87)

From about 1847 George Eyre designed encaustic tile pavements for Minton & Co. Later he worked with the Hill Pottery in Burslem and for a short time became art director at Copeland.

John Eyre (1847-1927)

Like many of his fellow designers, John Eyre began his career at Mintons' Art Pottery Studio before moving to Copeland where he worked as a designer for six years (c 1874-80). In 1885 he joined Doulton's Lambeth Studio and specialized in the design and painting of tile panels with J. H. McLennan and others.

Gordon Mitchell Forsyth (1879-1952)

At the age of twenty-four, Gordon Forsyth became art director at Minton Hollins & Co. where he stayed for two years before accepting a similar position at Pilkingtons Tile & Pottery Co. Although he was mainly involved in the production of Lancastrian ware, he was personally responsible for some magnificent tile panels, and under his direction, the company manufactured some of the best-known examples of English Art Nouveau tiling.

Herbert Wilson Foster (1848-1929)

Like many of his contemporaries, H. W. Foster studied at the Hanley and Kensington Schools of Art. He worked at Mintons for over twenty years, specializing in portraits and figure studies, some of which were executed on tiles.

George Goldie (1828-87)

George Goldie was in architectural practice with M. E. Hadfield. He designed pavements and tiles for Maw & Co. whose products he specified extensively for use in his buildings. He also accepted commissions for tiled pavements from Craven Dunnill.

260-261. "Summer" and "Winter" from a series of tiles produced by T. & R. Boote. Design attributed to Kate Greenaway c 1880.

Kate Greenaway (1846-1901)

Kate Greenaway's association with tile design began in 1864 while still a student at the Art Department of South Kensington. In 1868 she first exhibited a series of drawings on wood-blocks and subsequently went on to become one of the most successful and influential children's book illustrators of her day. Her close attention to detail blended well with an aesthetic stylishness and her delicate, carefully drawn children attracted many imitators. Her designs were ideally suited to tiles: they were flat, easy to comprehend and free of any complex shading. Several manufacturers produced tiles emulating the classic Greenaway style. T. & R. Boote registered a series of tiles illustrating the four seasons which are generally attributed to Kate Greenaway. In the same year they also registered several other tile designs illustrating typical Greenaway children at play.

262. Pattern card from the *Natural History* series by one of the Henks c 1882.

Christian Henk (1821-1905)

A ceramic decorator, Henk worked at Mintons from about 1848, where he specialized in Watteau figures and landscapes. Several sets of tile designs at Mintons labelled "Henk" are either the work of Christian Henk, or his son, John.

John Henk (1846-1914)

John Henk served his apprenticeship at Mintons and later became head modeller. His particular interest was in majolica and he probably designed many of Mintons' relief tiles decorated with majolica glazes.

Owen Jones (1809-74)

Like many of the early encaustic tile designers, Owen Jones was primarily an architect. His design philosophy was that ornament should be based on established geometric principles. Though he designed some tiles for Mintons, he worked mainly with Maw & Co.

263-274. Patterns for *Signs of the Zodiac* by H. Stacey Marks *c* 1880.

275. The pattern for "The Lean and Slippered Pantaloon" from the *Seven Ages of Man* series by H. Stacey Marks *c* 1882.

Henry Stacey Marks (1829-98)

Stacey Marks was a free-lance designer and painter who was commissioned by Mintons around 1871, though the majority of his tile designs date from about 1873. In that year, his plaques depicting the seven ages of man, painted at the Art Pottery Studio, were shown at the Vienna exhibition, where they were highly acclaimed. He also worked for Robert Minton Taylor, for whom he designed and painted several tile panels depicting female figures, and two interesting series *The Signs of the Zodiac* and *Aesop's Fables*. Since Mintons bought Taylor out in 1874, all the tile designs would have become the property of the new owners, and this may explain the origins of two Minton series, hitherto unattributed, illustrating the signs of the zodiac and Aesop's fables. Marks's designs, many of which are semi-humorous, are often finely balanced between medieval and Renaissance influence and are strongly aesthetic in approach.

101

276. Detail from Harrods Food Hall panel designed by W.J. Neatby 1902.

J. H. McLennan (fl. <u>c</u> 1879-1910)

McLennan was one of several artists employed by Doulton & Co. on the production of tile panels. He was involved in both designing and painting. Examples of his work include several panels in Lloyds Bank, Fleet Street, depicting scenes from Ben Jonson plays; and the interior of Queen Alexandra's house, Kensington Gore, where he worked, together with J. Eyre and others, on twelve panels illustrating notable figures from the history of music and ceramics.

William Morris (1834-96)

In 1856 Morris joined the thriving architectural practice of G. E. Street as a pupil, and there became acquainted with Philip Webb. Under the spell of the Pre-Raphaelite movement, and Rossetti's

102

277. Tile designed by E. J. Poynter for the Grill Room at the Victoria and Albert Museum 1868, 10 in × 10 in (26 cm × 26 cm).

influence in particular, Morris abandoned architecture for painting and design. In spite of his extraordinary prowess in virtually everything he turned his hand to — wallpapers, fabrics, book illustration, tapestries, carpets, printing and writing — he designed very few tiles. Most of the tile designs from Morris & Co. were undertaken by Burne-Jones. Of those that Morris is known to have designed, the majority were rather conventional, simple floral patterns. His designs were used as surrounds for the more ornate panels of Burne-Jones and other Morris & Co. designers.

William J. Neatby (1860-1910)

Neatby joined Doulton in 1890 where he went on to take charge of the architectural department. He left the company in 1907. He had no formal art training save that of a few years' work for an architect. From there he worked at Burmantofts in Leeds where he learned his trade in ceramics. At Doulton he was able to pursue his interests in different glazes and techniques of colouring, and introduced many original design methods that were unique to Doulton. He was a prolific designer and painter of tile panels, mostly in Art Nouveau and Pre-Raphaelite styles. Much of his work has been destroyed, but of those panels that still survive, probably the most well known are those in Harrods Meat Hall (1902) where there are twenty large Art Nouveau inspired panels depicting hunting and herding scenes, and many smaller panels showing a wide variety of game birds. He was also responsible for the panels in the Winter Gardens, Blackpool (1896), where there were twenty-eight panels with life-size paintings of girls in Pre-Raphaelite costumes. Possibly his most "notorious" achievement was the Everard Building in Bristol (1901) which created something of a stir at its unveiling being the first building to have polychrome ceramics as external decoration; its large-scale ceramic mural is symbolic of the craft of the printer.

Sir Edward John Poynter (1836-1919)

In 1861, after studying art in England and Paris, Poynter exhibited his first painting at the Royal Academy. During his career he designed frescos, mosaics, stained glass, pottery and tiles. Of the latter, he is best remembered for his grandiose tiled scheme in the Grill Room at the Victoria and Albert Museum (originally called the South Kensington Museum), consisting of large panels illustrating the seasons and months of the year above a dado of 10 in (25 cm) tiles depicting many different subjects, including figures, ships, landscapes, fruit and flowers. The tiles were designed between 1869 and 1870, and painted at Mintons' Art Pottery Studio in Kensington. In 1894 he was appointed Director of the National Gallery; and in 1896 he was elected President of the Royal Academy.

Augustus Welby Northmore Pugin (1812-52)

Pugin was instrumental in the reinstatement of the encaustic tile as a major part of English architectural decoration. As a Roman

278. Panel by Albert Slater 1895.

Catholic architect, he was largely responsible for the revival of interest in Gothic architecture and during his short career, he played the major role in well over one hundred buildings. He formed a close friendship with Herbert Minton, and the majority of his buildings completed after 1840 feature encaustic tiles made by Minton, to his own designs.

Halsey Ricardo (1854-1928)

Ricardo spent three formative years in Italy studying architecture and eventually became a pupil and assistant to Basil Champneys. The turning point in his career arose out of a meeting with William De Morgan which culminated in 1888 with a partnership between the two men. With the extra capital generated by the partnership, Ricardo designed and built the new Sands End Pottery in Fulham. While De Morgan was in Florence, Ricardo managed the factory

279. *Idylls of the King* by J. Moyr Smith. Mintons China Works *c* 1875.
280. *Theseus and the Crommyonian Sow* by J. Moyr Smith. Minton Hollins *c* 1880.
281. *Waverley Novels* by J. Moyr Smith. Mintons China Works *c* 1878.

and designed most of the relief tiles. With the mounting pressures of his architectural practice and the difficulties of running the business in De Morgan's absence, coupled with the fact that he had recently taken on a post as instructor in architectural design at the Central School of Art and Crafts, Ricardo brought the partnership to an end in 1898. By now, though, he was convinced of the virtues of tiles as a medium for colourful and durable external decoration, and he and Walter Crane campaigned long and hard to get them accepted. Ricardo's theories were put into practice in Sir Ernest Debenham's house in Addison Road, Kensington, which was completed in 1907 and which was completely clad in glazed ceramics.

John Pollard Seddon (1827-1906)

Seddon is best known for his achievements as an architect but he also designed furniture and pottery, and was interested in lithography. In the 1870s he designed encaustic floor tiles for Maw & Co. and William Godwin & Sons.

Albert Slater (fl. <u>c</u> 1886)

Slater was an extremely skilled tile painter whose approach was more graphic than realistic. He undertook a considerable amount of work for Minton Hollins and Co. for which he produced large decorative panels ranging from Landseer-type animal studies to Victorian bathing scenes.

282. Design from the *Anacreon* series by J. Moyr Smith *c* 1878.

John Moyr Smith (fl. <u>c</u> 1872-89)

Moyr Smith worked for Mintons China Works where most of his energies were devoted to designing picture tiles. As a free-lance, he was able to work for Minton Hollins and W. B. Simpson & Sons and in all was responsible for more than twenty different series of transfer-printed picture tiles, some of which were printed in colour. He also had interests in book illustrations and furniture

105

283. *Old Testament* by J. Moyr Smith.
Mintons China Works *c* 1870.
284. "Cymbals" from the *Classical Musicians* series by J. Moyr Smith.
Mintons China Works *c* 1876.

285. *Spirit of the Flowers* by J. Moyr Smith. Mintons China Works *c* 1872.
286. *Fables* by J. Moyr Smith. Mintons China Works *c* 1872.

design. Moyr Smith sympathized with the Arts and Crafts Movement, but his designs retained a unique quality bordering on the classical.

Louis Marc Emmanuel Solon (1835-1913)

Louis Marc Solon came to Mintons in 1870 after training in Paris and at Sèvres, where he learnt the extremely difficult *pâte sur pâte* method of decoration which was to make him famous. Most of his *pâte sur pâte* works on plaques, vases and other wares include cherubs and diaphanously clad girls, subjects which responded well

287-289. *Industrial* by J. Moyr Smith. Mintons China Works *c* 1870.

290-291. Original designs for the *Cooking* series by L. M. Solon. Mintons China Works *c* 1882.

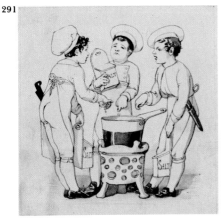

to the technique. He occasionally made plaques and tiles decorated in sgraffito. The only printed tiles that can be directly ascribed to him are a series of twelve tiles humorously treating the subject of cooking which are a complete departure from his usual romantic style. He left Mintons in 1904 but continued to work for them on a free-lance basis.

Louis Solon also wrote extensively on many aspects of ceramics.

Leon Victor Solon (1872-1957)

Leon Victor Solon attended Hanley and Kensington Schools of Art before following in the footsteps of his father and joining Mintons in 1896. By 1900 he was art director of the firm. He specialized in slip-trailed Art Nouveau design and was probably responsible for the majority of Mintons' Art Nouveau tiles. Many of his hand-painted tile panels were inspired by the works of Alphonse Mucha, though he was more successful with the Secessionist wares that he and John Wadsworth introduced to Mintons in 1902. In 1909 Solon emigrated to America where he embarked on a successful career in the American tile industry.

George Edmund Street (1824-81)

Though George Street designed tiled pavements for Maw & Co. between 1855 and 1870, he is best remembered as an architect, writer and designer who fostered many of the leading figures in the Arts and Crafts Movement. He employed William Morris for a short time in 1856. In 1881 Street became president of the Royal Institute of British Architects.

Charles H. Temple (1857-1940)

Temple was the principal designer at Maw & Co. between 1887 and 1907. He was instrumental in squeezing out the free-lance designers and was emphatic that tile designs should be the work of factory staff only, so Walter Crane, Lewis Day and others, ceased to work for the company from about 1890 though their designs were still used. Temple was a prolific and versatile designer. At the Chicago World Fair in 1893, Maw's highly successful exhibits were largely the result of his endeavours.

107

292

292. *Bird and Tree* designed by C. F. A. Voysey. Maw & Co. *c* 1898. Tube lined.

Margaret Thompson (fl. <u>c</u> 1890-1930)

Margaret Thompson's best-known works are the nursery rhyme and other similar children's panels executed by Doulton & Co. early this century. Working closely with her colleague William Rowe, she designed and painted many large panels intended for use in hospital wards. No two panels of the same subject were identical, since the design and technique were changed slightly for each commission. Most of them are signed M.T. and W.R. in the bottom corners.

Charles Francis Annesley Voysey (1857-1941)

Voysey was another architect who turned his attention to the decorative arts. He joined the Art Workers Guild in 1884. By the turn of the century, he had completed his own house, and it was probably while working on the furnishings that he became involved with tile design. He became one of Pilkingtons' major design consultants and was responsible for such popular patterns as "Tulip Tree", "Fish and Leaf", "Bird and Lemon Tree" and "Vine and Bird", many of which utilized his favoured Art Nouveau heart-shaped motif. In 1924 he became master of the Art Workers Guild. His influence was felt well into the first quarter of this century, not least on thousands of houses built in the 1930s which

293. *Animal Groups* by William Wise.
Mintons China Works *c* 1883.
294. *Village Life* by William Wise.
Mintons China Works *c* 1882.
295. Original drawing for the *Country Pursuits* series by William Wise.
Mintons China Works *c* 1886.

have roofs that sweep down to the bedroom windows and are detailed to give a dormer effect — a technique Voysey first used in 1888.

William Wise (1847-89)

William Wise turned his attention to etching and engraving while still attending art school. Having acquired these technical skills, he entered the world of industrial design, where he achieved considerable success. His early work displays the contemporary interest in the Renaissance. His output of tile designs was considerable and he was responsible for at least six series including several landscapes. Not all of Mintons' landscape tiles can be attributed to Wise, however, since L. T. Swetnam was responsible for some and his initials are occasionally found on tiles which in the past have been attributed to Wise. Their two styles are almost indistinguishable and it may be that Swetnam took over when Wise died and continued working in the same style, as most designs initialled LTS seem to date from about 1890, the year after Wise died.

Philip Webb (1831-1915)

Webb became principal assistant to G. E. Street in 1852. In 1859 he established his own practice and one of his first commissions was the design of William Morris's Red House in 1860. He was slowly drawn into the embryonic Morris, Marshall, Faulkner & Co. where he became responsible for most of the furniture design. He is only known to have designed one set of tiles while with the company: a series of birds painted in pale blues.

Sir Matthew Digby Wyatt (1820-77)

Matthew Digby Wyatt, the eminent Victorian architect and writer on architectural design and ornament, extended his interests to the study of geometric mosaics of the Middle Ages, which culminated in a book on the subject being published in 1848. He later designed encaustic and mosaic floors for Maw & Co.

109

CHAPTER FIVE

Photographic and Portrait Tiles

In July 1897 an advertisement appeared in the *Pottery Gazette*, which read, "At last, Photo Decorated Tiles". This was the culmination of many months' effort by George Grundy of Derby, but it was not the first successful attempt to decorate a ceramic tile with a photographic image.

Ferdinand Jean Joubert de la Ferté took out a patent in 1860 for "Improvements in reproducing photographs and other pictures, on the surface of glass or ceramic". Obviously attempts had already been made to fix a photographic image to a ceramic surface. At a time when photographs were highly susceptible to fading, this offered security against the ravages of time and atmospheric change. Though his process worked well, it was not suited to mass production, and it remained the province of Joubert and his contemporaries for the benefit of their richer clients.

Joubert's success encouraged others to intensify their efforts to produce a commercially viable method and in 1876 John Henry Johnson filed a patent which drew heavily on Joubert's technique, but which was to become the basis of commercial practice. "Photo Chrosie", as he termed it, was suited to decorating earthenware and porcelain, and could be applied to both glazed and unglazed surfaces. The major advantage of photochrosie was that it could be applied to curved as well as flat surfaces and hence was a much more attractive propostion to the china manufacturers.

A cleaned copper plate was coated with a light-sensitive emulsion. After exposure, the plate was dusted with vitrifiable metallic powder, which stuck to the exposed parts of the image. The powdering could be repeated several times until a perfect image was obtained, thus allowing precise control of the image quality. When fully "developed" the plate was coated with well-filtered collodion, which held the powder image in position while the plate was thoroughly washed to remove all traces of the light-sensitive coating. The collodion support, together with the image it contained, was then lifted from the plate and transferred to the article it was to decorate — powder side out. During firing, the collodion was destroyed, leaving behind the vitrified image. This "dusting-on" process as it became known, continued to be refined through the 1880s even to the point of three-colour printing and a technique which involved hand colouring of the printed photographic image, which went under the exotic title of

296. Photographic tile by the dusting-on process. The photograph is of a popular painting *Ariadne c* 1890.

Photo Diaphano Chromogram. By 1895 the dusting-on technique was the standard method employed, and was used with some success by firms like Mintons.

The majority of the photographic tiles in circulation, and it must be remembered that we are talking of a very small percentage of the total Victorian tile output, were made on mass-produced tile blanks and plaques by photographers who were used to dealing with the chemicals involved and to working under the stringent conditions the process called for — one speck of dust could ruin the whole effect. Of course, the average photographer did not have a kiln in his workshop and so companies were formed which, in addition to supplying all the requisites for the process, offered a firing service to the photographer. This meant that he could simply apply the image to the tile and send it off to be fired. The Midland Photo Depot in Hanley, the Photo Keramic Co. in Nottingham, J. G. Tunny & Co. of Edinburgh all specialized in this sort of work.

Another contemporary technique, which involved platinum or gold toning a collodion positive stripped from its support, was known as the substitution process. Here the silver in a normal photographic transparency was replaced by gold or platinum in the toning bath. This technique was expensive but yielded unsurpassable results. A rather different method of decoration, but which also relied on a photographic image was the Autotype process, or Collotype as it later became known.

Josiah Wedgwood & Sons was among the first companies to adopt the new process in the 1870s. It was a lithographic process in which a stone was coated with a light-sensitive emulsion and exposed to light through a negative. After exposure, the image was developed by washing in cold water, and later dried. The image that remained varied in hardness according to the amount of light that had passed through the negative and when dampened, would selectively absorb or reject water according to its hardness, so that when the plate was inked, a print could be taken off which had full tonal values. The inks used had a large proportion of vitrifiable powder in them so that when the print was transferred to the ware and fired, a permanent image remained.

Drawing to some extent on each of the foregoing methods, George Grundy in 1896 applied for patent protection for his method of decorating ceramic ware. Grundy was a photographer by profession, and together with his colleague George Lingard, a Collotype printer, invested a substantial amount of money in the venture. Their method, which was suitable for under or overglaze decoration, involved spreading a light-sensitive coating over a flexible rubber support and exposing it to a suitable negative. After subsequent development and treatment as for the Collotype process, the flexible plate was inked with a specially prepared solution containing the vitrifiable colour and printed directly onto the tile. In order to build up the required depth of ink to withstand the firing process, several impressions had to be made on the tile in

exact register. To ensure successful results, Grundy had to carefully select a tile biscuit which was porous enough both to accept the ink and be ready for another impression immediately afterwards. To this end he chose tiles by Maw & Co. The method was by far the cheapest of the various processes available and the tiles enjoyed moderate success during the few months they were in production. Operating as the Photo Decorated Tile Co. from a factory in Tutbury, near Derby, George Grundy concentrated his efforts solely on the production of these tiles, and his first catalogue boasted sixty different subjects: views of famous resorts, printed in monochrome on a cream or white background.

With the perfection of the half-tone printing process in 1888, tile manufacturers had a golden opportunity to improve on the traditional methods of etching and engraving copper plates for use in transfer printing, but it was not until ten years later that C. H. Temple of Maw & Co. patented a method of transfer-printing tile designs from a photographic half-tone plate.

The usual method of printing from a half-tone block was to take an impression from the raised surface of the plate, but Temple filled the sunken areas with colour and scraped the top surface clean. The print could then be taken and applied to the tile. This technique produced good quality transfer prints with a full tonal range, at a fraction of the cost of conventionally prepared prints, and marked the beginning of the end for wholly hand-worked, transfer-printed designs.

113

299-300. "Gladstone" by George Cartlidge. Sherwin & Cotton c 1897-1924. The red glaze detracts from the photographic effect. The darker tile looks more authentic despite the loss of detail.

Portrait Tiles and the George Cartlidge Controversy

301. Hand-painted by George Cartlidge c 1895.

George Cartlidge was responsible for one of the most enduring controversies in English tile production. The tiles he produced for Sherwin & Cotton, J. H. Barratt & Co., and others, bear an uncanny resemblance to photographs; so much so, that they have fallen under the generic term "Photographic Tiles". Cartlidge himself was adamant that the tiles were completely hand modelled and not manufactured under any photographic process, though he did concede that many of his portraits were copied from photographs. His Abraham Lincoln tile is inscribed "In commemoration of the 100th anniversary celebration of the birth of Abraham Lincoln, February 12th 1909, modelled from the only untouched negative in the United States, taken in 1864". Several other tiles also refer to the original portrait. There are arguments for both the hand modelled and photographic theories; the wealth of detail and tonal values contained in some of the tiles suggest that the tiles are photographically derived, possibly by photomechanical etching of a master metal plate, from which the die could be made to produce the tile. In order to obtain the varying degrees of relief, the plate would have to have been etched several times, masking off the raised areas between successive applications of the etchant — leading to a well-defined line between areas of high and low relief, which would have ruined the whole effect. So were the tiles hand modelled? If they were, then Cartlidge must have suddenly developed an extraordinary ability to copy photographs accurately as his paintings on china and canvas reveal an artist rather simplistic in approach. It may be that the original portrait was photographically printed onto a clay tablet, and using the image as

301

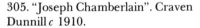

302. "Matene Te Nga" by George Cartlidge. Sherwin & Cotton c 1897-1924.

303. "Abraham Lincoln" by George Cartlidge. Sherwin & Cotton c 1897-1924.

304. "Queen Victoria" by George Cartlidge. Sherwin & Cotton c 1897-1924.

305. "Joseph Chamberlain". Craven Dunnill c 1910.

an extremely accurate guide, the portrait was hand modelled. However the tiles were modelled, they do prove that Cartlidge had a good working knowledge of the technique known as *émaux ombrants*. Here, the original model was done in clay, from which a plaster cast would be taken and finally a metal die made from which the tile would be produced. The realization of the photographic effect now lay in the application of the glaze. With a normal relief tile the glaze was run as evenly as possible over the whole surface but in this technique the glaze was allowed to pond in the deeper areas and to run off the raised areas, producing the shading effect. Once the glaze had been applied, the tile had to be fired absolutely flat or the glaze would run off to one side of the tile, leaving a thick band of colour down one side, a fault which commonly occurs on these tiles.

In an attempt to emulate Cartlidge's success, most companies introduced a range of portrait tiles, with varying degrees of success. Carter & Co. produced a series of World War I celebrities, but perhaps the most successful alternative to Cartlidge's portraits were those produced by Craven Dunnill. Its series included Edward VII and Queen Alexandra, Joseph Chamberlain, and Ramsay MacDonald. In addition to these, Craven Dunnill introduced a series of modelled portraits, as did J. C. Edwards, Maw, Mintons and most of the major manufacturers. Those modelled by Craven Dunnill include Shakespeare, Chaucer, Longfellow, General Gordon, and Gladstone. J. C. Edwards modelled Lord Salisbury and Queen Victoria. Malkin Edge & Co. also produced tiles of Longfellow and Shakespeare, and other famous writers.

Transfer-printed portrait tiles were also produced. Queen Victoria is well represented on tiles by Mintons and Minton Hollins; a Copeland & Garrett tile depicts John Bull "extinguishing a firebrand" and a series by Wedgwood illustrates Charles Dickens, William Shakespeare, and Charles Swinburne. Wedgwood also made an Edward VII tile which often appears as a teapot stand.

CHAPTER SIX

Art Nouveau and After

When in 1895 Samuel Bing, the noted German art dealer, opened 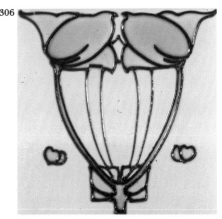 his shop in Paris, he unwittingly gave a name to the powerful movement which was growing around him in the field of the decorative arts. "La Maison de l'Art Nouveau" was opened to sell oriental art, but almost straight away moved into selling the best of the new decorative arts for interior decoration: furniture, paintings, glass, textiles and tiles. The seeds of the Art Nouveau movement were planted with the Pre-Raphaelites but it was only with William Morris and his followers that it began to germinate, finally blossoming into the sensuous sweeping lines of High Art Nouveau which reached its peak at the Paris Exhibition of 1900. No previous movement exerted as much influence; Art Nouveau reached into the homes of the poorest workers and into the palaces of the richest kings. To the tile manufacturers, the advent of Art Nouveau was heaven sent. They relied heavily on changes in taste, and interest in tiles was beginning to wane. Several struggling companies revived, other new ones were founded. Unfortunately, some companies had not learned the lessons of the 1850s, and produced inferior design on poor quality tiles. The main cause for complaint was that some designers, overwhelmed with their new found freedom, had returned to producing tiles that could only be used in isolation, so that rather than selling more of these highly decorative, well proportioned tiles, the companies were in fact selling less, though there was a corresponding rise in sales of plain tiles which were used to show off the decorative tile to the best effect. After the initial euphoria had died down, the public became more selective in its choice of tile, and tile design started to improve. During the period 1898 to 1906 many designs were registered at the Patent Office, particularly by the Henry Richards Tile Co. and to a lesser extent by the Rhodes Tile Co., J. & W. Wade, H. A. Ollivant and Pilkingtons. By the turn of the century tube lining became more popular than ever before, which led to the widespread adoption of a mechanical substitute and many so-called "tube line" tiles were made by machine pressing. With the exception of Mintons China Works few manufacturers made tiles with printed Art Nouveau motifs. In general the Art Nouveau motifs responded better to the three-dimensional treatment of an impressed tile decorated in majolica glazes.

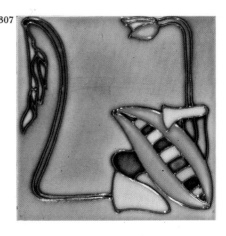

306-307. Art Nouveau tube lining c 1900.

Of all the tile manufacturers, only Pilkingtons had the foresight to commission designs by the pioneers of the movement: Walter Crane, Lewis Day, C. F. A. Voysey and Alphonse Mucha. Some of their designs were mass produced, particularly those by Lewis Day and Voysey, while others were hand painted by skilled artists. Walter Crane, who categorically denied any involvement with Art Nouveau, created *Flora's Train*, a series of six tube-line tiles which became the model for the stylized interpretation of the female form throughout the whole Art Nouveau movement. The Czech artist Alphonse Mucha, well known for his poster design for Sarah Bernhardt, designed a series of four tile panels which echoed his work on posters and which again became a model for contemporary artists to draw on. C. F. A. Voysey, despite calling Art Nouveau

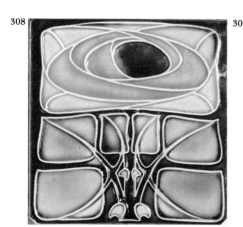

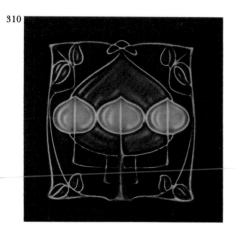

308 and 310. Typical Art Nouveau tiles *c* 1898-1910. (308) H. Richards Tile Co. (310) Corn Bros.

309. Art Nouveau tiling. Café Lipp, Paris 1900.

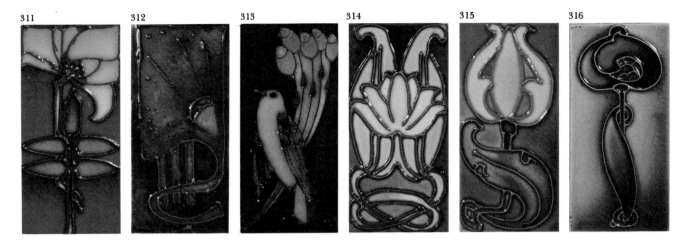

"an unhealthy and revolting style", created some of the most distinctive and enduring work of the period. He was strongly influenced by Arthur Heygate Mackmurdo who had also been a disciple of William Morris. Mackmurdo's emphasis on narrow vertical line can be seen on much of Voysey's work in furniture, interior design and tiles.

Another eminent designer who was strongly influenced by Mackmurdo was Charles Rennie Mackintosh, who, though not directly involved in tile design, was instrumental in establishing the Glasgow School of Art Nouveau design. He was the creator of a new rectilinear approach to Art Nouveau which shunned the sweeping, sinuous lines and personification of plant forms, and concentrated on the functional straight line — long and narrow to emphasize compensating gentle curves. It was some time before this approach was applied to tilework in England although it was popular on the Continent.

Art Nouveau motifs started to appear on tiles from about 1897, but enjoyed their greatest popularity just after the turn of the century. At this time virtually all the mass-produced tiles were impressed and decorated in majolica glazes, most commonly with a stylized floral motif: lilies, inspired by Rossetti's early paintings, orchids and other exotic flowers. Tightly formed flowers such as roses did not become popular until the rectilinear phase of Art Nouveau became accepted and they could be incorporated into a more geometric linear pattern. To the designers, working to try

311-316. Tube-lined Art Nouveau tiles by various manufacturers c 1900.

317-319. Art Nouveau tiles 1898-1910. (317) Probably Pilkingtons. (318) T. A. Simpson. (319) H. A. Ollivant.

317

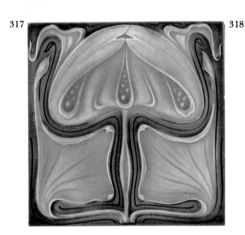

318

319

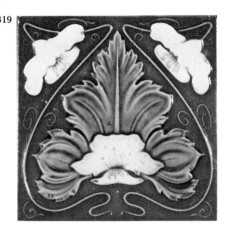

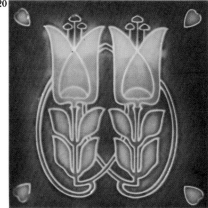

320

320-324. More Art Nouveau tiles
1898-1910. (320) H. Richards Tile Co.
(321) A large plastic-clay plaque by
Mintons China Works 1898. (322) H.
Richards Tile Co. (323 and 324)
Gibbons Hinton.

321

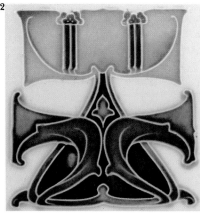

322

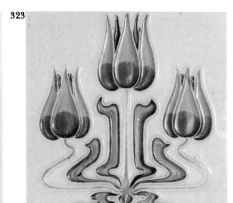

323

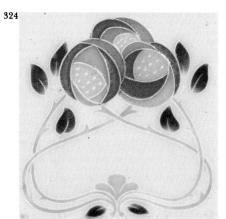

324

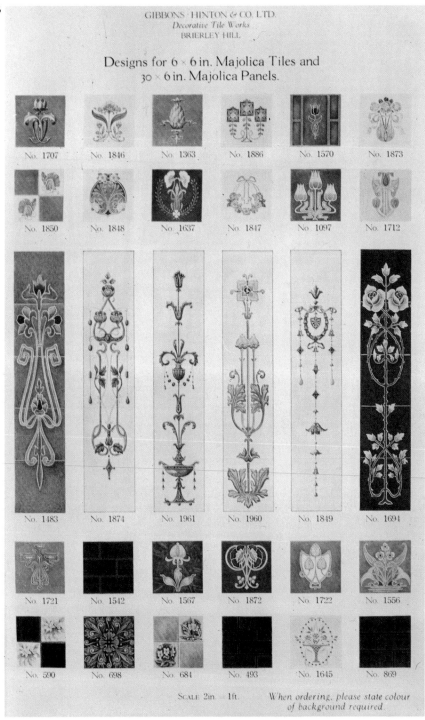

and fill a 6 in (15 cm) square, the long-stemmed flowers with leaves that could be made to flow and curve were ideal, and so tulips, irises and poppies were increasingly used particularly by the Richards Tile Co.

By 1910 Art Nouveau was in decline and in the vacuum created by its demise many of the newer companies closed down; others like Mintons China Works stopped tile manufacture in favour of its other interests. Tile design tended to revert to the styles of the 1860s.

The economic conditions prevailing at the time and the onset of

World War 1 further retarded the development of tile design, but with the arrival of peace and improving standards of living, another form of decorative art was emerging: Art Deco. Fashion designer Paul Poiret exerted a profound influence over Parisian fashion and interior design, and by 1920 Paris was the undisputed centre of this new movement in decorative art. By 1925, after the

326-327. Early Art Deco panels in the Michelin Building, London. Produced by Gillardoni Fils & Cie and designed by Edouard Montaud 1910. 326 depicts motoring pioneer Edward VII (left).

326

327

Exposition Internationale des Arts Decoratifs et Industriels Modernes, Art
Deco had reached its peak.

At the same time, another school of thought was emerging opposed to Poiret's ideals of stylized elegance. Le Corbusier and his circle built on the precepts laid down by Mackintosh and sought a purity of line unhampered by irrelevant and distracting detail. From these two points of view, emerged a synthesized style of decoration based on geometric and formalized design motifs tempered by the Cubist emphasis on line and colour.

Surprisingly, the tile manufacturers remained aloof to the possibilities offered by Art Deco, and only a handful were prepared to commit themselves to large scale involvement. Maw & Co. and Craven Dunnill both produced some interesting work based on the strong geometric principles of Art Deco, and the use  of a light relief together with egg-shell glazes, some of which had a curious metallic sheen in them, gave their tiles a quality which was wholly in keeping with the decorative schemes of the time. To find out why the majority of the tile companies avoided Art Deco design one has to consider the domestic environment. This was a time when whole living areas were influenced by Art Deco: from their furniture and lighting to cutlery and crockery. To have a room in which every tile bore a strong decorative motif would have been unbearable, and so in general a decorative tile was used as part of an overall plain-coloured scheme; if two hundred tiles were used in the kitchen, perhaps ten of them would be decorated. This sort of scheme would serve to highlight the decorated tiles without overwhelming the other decorative features of the room.

To some tile manufacturers, this limited use of decorated tiles meant that they became uneconomic to produce, and so they turned their production effort over to the manufacture of plain tiles and the new slabbed fireplaces that were becoming fashionable. These fireplaces were built on a concrete slab that was tiled at the factory and simply screwed or cemented in place on site. The majority of the fireplaces were made of plain or mottled tiles in light pastel shades.

The one room where decorative tiles were used with relative abandon was the bathroom; here the walls could be covered with bright sparkling tiles without fear of detracting from the furniture. Chrome fittings and large mirrors all contributed to the clean, vibrant effect.

After the exhibition of 1925, the passion for strong visual impact began to subside and an overall use of subdued colour together with a more gentle flowing approach to design, began to take its place. Printed and hand-painted tiles began to reappear, but in general, plain tiles were far more popular.

Between the wars prizes were offered for the imaginative use of tiling on building façades, and Doulton's Carraraware was used on an increasingly wide spectrum of cinemas, theatres, factories and other business premises, creating the evocative look of the thirties. World War II saw the end of the vogue for decorated tiles. Even post-war rebuilding failed to inspire a new source of design, and it was not until the mid-fifties that the decorated tile was revived,

328. Tube-lined tile by Pilkingtons *c* 1920.
329. Minton Hollins *c* 1925.

122

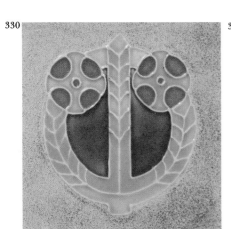

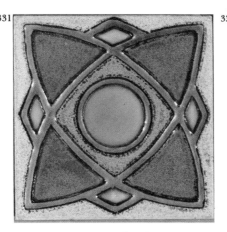

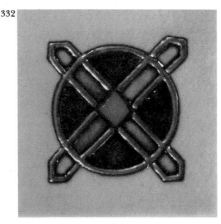

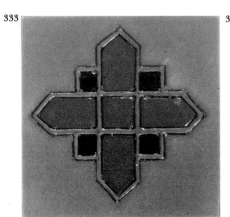

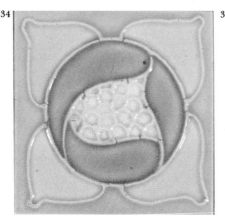

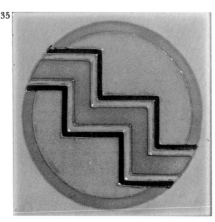

330-335. Maw & Co. Art Deco tiles in a variety of glazes c 1925.

screen printed and lithographed in the vivid colours that went with the widespread use of plastics in the home.

As Britain recovered from the effects of war, new export markets were explored and overseas contracts won, but tiles were heavy and cumbersome, and apart from the physical difficulties of shipping, some countries imposed heavy import duties on the weight of goods brought into the country. The tile manufacturers had to take a hard look at their products, and after much experimentation, came up with a new breed of thinner and much lighter tile. The import duties were no longer a problem and the spin-off for the home market was considerable. With a lighter tile, one could use a lighter adhesive which meant that tiling was made much easier. Tiling became the province of the home handyman, and with this revolutionary step, the tile industry secured its continued prosperity.

336-338. Hand-painted on Maw & Co. blanks. Attributed to John Pearson c 1930.

123

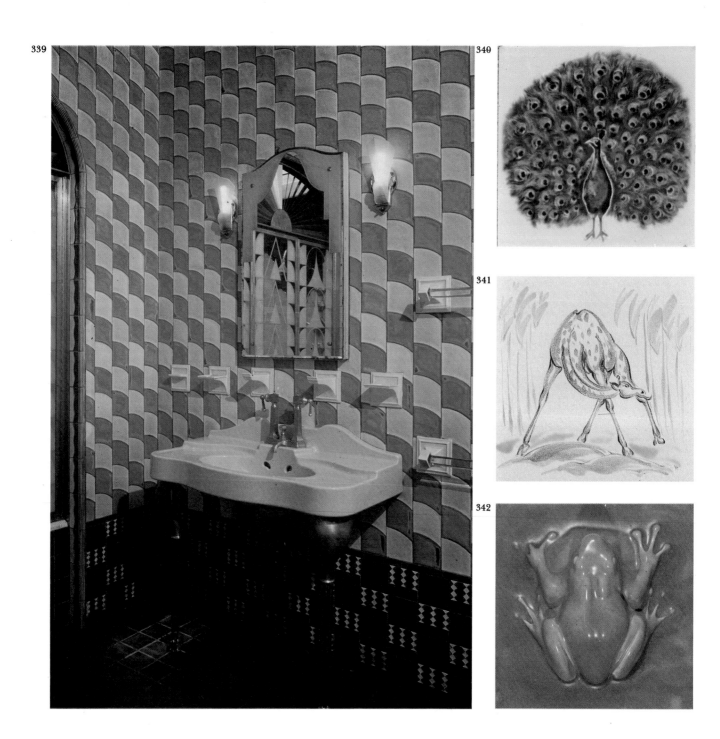

Today's decorative tiles are still made by the same basic techniques and are as popular as they were in the 1880s, though they are used with more restraint and understanding. In recent years there has been a return to some of the more popular Victorian approaches to design. Tube lining is gaining in popularity and some of the original Victorian designs are being used in their entirety. The current interest in restoring Victorian property resulted in H. & R. Johnson Ltd. being approached to manufacture encaustic tiles. Unfortunately the art had been lost when Art Nouveau was at its height. Herbert Minton would have been intrigued to learn that 140 years after he rediscovered the lost

339. 1930s Art Deco bathroom. Chanim Building, New York.
340. H. Richards Tile Co. c 1930.
341. Overglaze decoration on Pilkingtons blank c 1930.
342. High relief tile in "egg shell" glaze c 1930. Unattributed.

343. 1970s bathroom tile scheme
designed by Alison Britton.

art of encaustic tile making to repair medieval floors, another tile manufacturer was struggling with the same problems he faced, suffering the same disappointments, sharing the same triumphs, in order to repair the tiled floors that he had created.

Today H. & R. Johnson and Pilkingtons dominate the decorative tile industry, but within them the names of many of the old companies live on. Every tile they make, whether it is a wall or a floor tile, decorative or plain, bears tribute to the skill and tenacity of their Victorian forefathers who gave the world a new and enduring branch of the decorative arts.

344-346. 1970s Pilkingtons tiles.

125

APPENDIX A

Identifying and Dating Tiles

The identification of tiles, even marked examples, can create a great many problems for the unwary collector. Any mark on the back of the tile may well point to a manufacturer who was responsible for both the tile biscuit and the design on it. However, there were a great many tile decorators like W. B. Simpson, and Shrigley & Hunt, who used bought-in tile blanks upon which they printed or painted their own designs. W. B. Simpson used Mintons' and Maw's tiles extensively, but occasionally tiles are found with Simpson's own mark impressed in the back, indicating that the company had the tile biscuit made for it, probably by Maw, as it had no manufacturing facilities of its own. Tile decorations by Shrigley & Hunt are found on a wide variety of marked tile backs, but in the majority of cases it used Copeland tiles. The Decorative Art Tile Co. used ready-made blanks from other companies, as well as having its own impressed tiles made by another manufacturer. In addition to the professional decorators, there were a great many amateurs who either hand painted their own designs, or hand tinted ready-printed outlines on tiles purchased from a local stockist.

Even when a tile has a popular design printed on it, problems arise. Take *Industrial*, for example, designed by Moyr Smith for Mintons China Works. This is usually found on Mintons China Works' tiles, either marked with the name or having a familiar back pattern. But occasionally this pattern is found with a Doulton stamp printed on the back; most probably because Doulton liked the design and sold it alongside their own wares.

To further complicate matters, it was quite usual for manufacturers to purchase another's tile blanks and print their own design on it, either because of a shortfall in production or because they felt that someone else's tiles were more suited for a particular job.

Having explained the problems that face the collector, we can go on and look at the marks found on tile backs. To make things difficult, a great many tiles are anonymous, they have no maker's name or even a trade mark on the back. In some cases it is possible to establish a link between the pattern on the back and a particular manufacturer, but here again, the pattern was not the sole prerogative of any particular manufacturer, and many used the same design.

The pattern was formed on the back for one reason alone — to provide a key for the mortar when fixing. For tiles that were to be fixed in hazardous situations patented lock or safety backs were developed where slots in the back of the tile were undercut so that the wet mortar would press into the tile body and form a dovetail. Sherwin & Cotton's patent lock back, Doulton & Co.'s safety back and Maw & Co.'s double grip back are good examples of this kind of safety device. The comb back on the plastic-clay tiles of Copeland, Burmantofts, Pilkingtons and others, automatically formed a lock back because of the ridges and angles formed when the comb was pulled through.

To be able to identify the maker of a tile, a certain amount of care and judgment must be exercised when trying to date it from the marks on the back, as they may pre-date the actual tile design by several years, either because the tile was made and stored away for some time before use, or because the old metal dies were still in use long after a new trade mark or back stamp was introduced. Equally, the design may well pre-date the tile as instanced by several of Wedgwood's designs which were used on tableware long before their application to tiles. However, it is possible to combine information from the back of the tile with the style of decoration and techniques used on the front, and arrive at a fairly accurate date. Some tiles are dated, and many have a system of dots and letters forming a date code, but the majority of these have still to be decoded. Registration numbers provide clues as to when the designs were first registered and by whom. But a design first registered in 1860 could easily still be in production thirty years later, and not necessarily by the same manufacturer, as the original manufacturer may have sold the rights, or, as is more likely, the design was "borrowed" when the protection expired.

Other clues to the date of a tile are listed below.

(A) The word "England" is often found on tiles and signifies that the tile was made after 1891, and was intended for export. The absence of the word, however, does not imply that the tile pre-dated 1891.

(B) "Made in England" denotes a tile made after 1900 — again its absence does not imply the tile was made before 1900.

(C) A trade mark, either impressed or printed, signifies a date after 1862 when the Trade Marks Act was introduced. The words "Trade Mark" in conjunction with the actual mark indicate a date after 1875.

(D) Any abbreviation of the word "Limited" must be after 1860, but more likely after 1880.

(E) Impressed letters and numbers can sometimes be found on tiles made by Copeland between 1870 and 1969, the letter denotes the month, and the numbers the last two figures of the year.
J = January, F = February, M = March, A = April, Y = May, U = June, L = July, T = August, S = September, O = October, N = November, D = December.

(F) From 1926 Pilkingtons used a letter to denote year of manufacture: P=1926, L='27, K='28, I='29, N='30, G='31,

127

T=''32, O=''33, S=''34, J=''35, E=''36, H=''37, D=''38, A=''39, V=''40, I=''41, B=''42, C=''43, D=''44, . . . to H=''48, J=''49, K=''50, . . . to Z=''65, A=''66, B=''67, . . . to H=''73, J=''74, K=''75, . . . to P=''80.

(G) From 1842 until 1883 many tiles were marked with a diamond to indicate that the design was registered and protected for three years:

1842-1867 Year Letter at Top		*1868-1883* Year Letter at Right	
A = 1845	N = 1864	A = 1871	V = 1876
B = 1858	O = 1862	C = 1870	W = (1-6 March)
C = 1844	P = 1851	D = 1878	1878
D = 1852	Q = 1866	E = 1881	X = 1868
E = 1855	R = 1861	F = 1873	Y = 1879
F = 1847	S = 1849	H = 1869	
G = 1863	T = 1867	I = 1872	
H = 1843	U = 1848	J = 1880	
I = 1846	V = 1850	K = 1883	
J = 1854	W = 1865	L = 1882	
K = 1857	X = 1842	P = 1877	
L = 1856	Y = 1853	S = 1875	
M = 1859	Z = 1860	U = 1874	

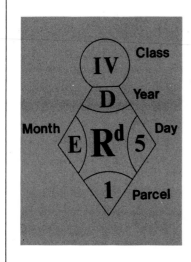

(e.g., 5 May 1852)

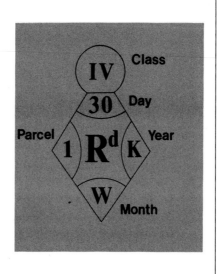

(e.g., 30 March 1883)

Months (both periods)

A = December	G = February	M = June
B = October	H = April	R = August (and
C or	I = July	1-19 September
O = January	K = November (and	1857)
D = September	December 1860)	W = March
E = May		

Design Registration Numbers 1884 to 1909

Rd. No. (Jan)

1884:	1-19753
1885:	19754-40479
1886:	40480-64519
1887:	64520-90482
1888:	90483-116647
1889:	116648-141272
1890:	141273-163766
1891:	163767-185712
1892:	185713-205239
1893:	205240-224719
1894:	224720-246974
1895:	246975-268391
1896:	268392-291240
1897:	291241-311657
1898:	311658-331706
1899:	331707-351201
1900:	351202-368153
1901:	368154-385499
1902:	385500-402499
1903:	402500-419999
1904:	420000-446999
1905:	447000-470999
1906:	471000-493999
1907:	494000-518999
1908:	519000-549999
1909:	550000

Tile Backs and Marks

The following drawings illustrate tile-back markings which can be attributed to particular companies and which indicate the dates when the tiles were in common use. It should be remembered that very few companies marked all their tiles and nearly all produced some tiles without distinctive back markings.

All marks are moulded or impressed except where otherwise stated.

Abbreviations

E — Encaustic
P — Plastic-clay tile
D — Dust-pressed tile
W — Wall tile
F — Floor tile

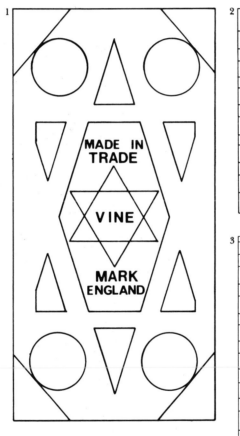

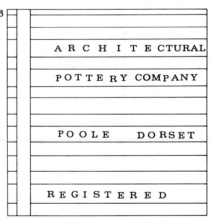

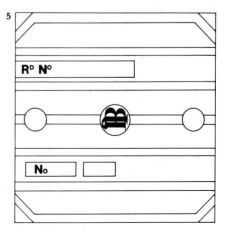

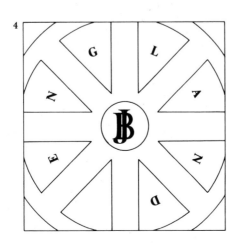

Adams & Cartlidge
(1)   1911-16   W.D.
Architectural Pottery Co.
(2)   1854-95   E.P.
(3)   1854-95   E.P.
J. H. Barratt & Co.
(4)   1900-25   W.D.
(5)   1895-1909   W.D.

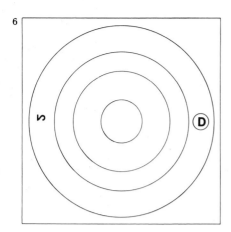

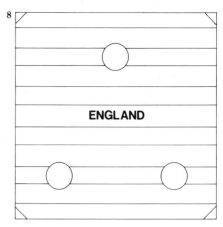

⁹T.G. & F.B.

¹² **BURMANTOFTS FAIENCE**

ENGLAND

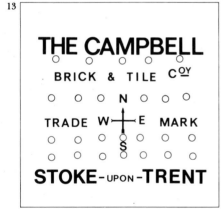

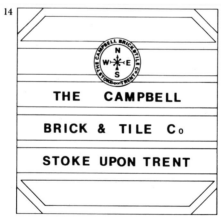

T. & R. Boote
(6)	*c* 1880-1910	W.D.
(7)	*c* 1862-1910	W.D.
(8)	*c* 1895-1910	W.D.

T. G. & F. Booth
(9)	1883-91	W.D.
	(printed mark)	

Brown, Westhead, Moore & Co.
(10)	1862-1904	W.D.

Burmantofts
(11)	1880-1904	W.P.
(12)	1891-1904	W.P.

Campbell Brick & Tile Co.
(13)	1875-82	E.P.
(14)	1875-82	W.D.
	(brick deleted after 1882)	
(15)	*c* 1930	W.D.

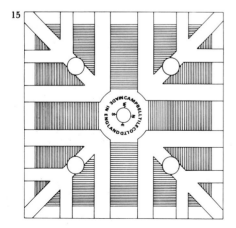

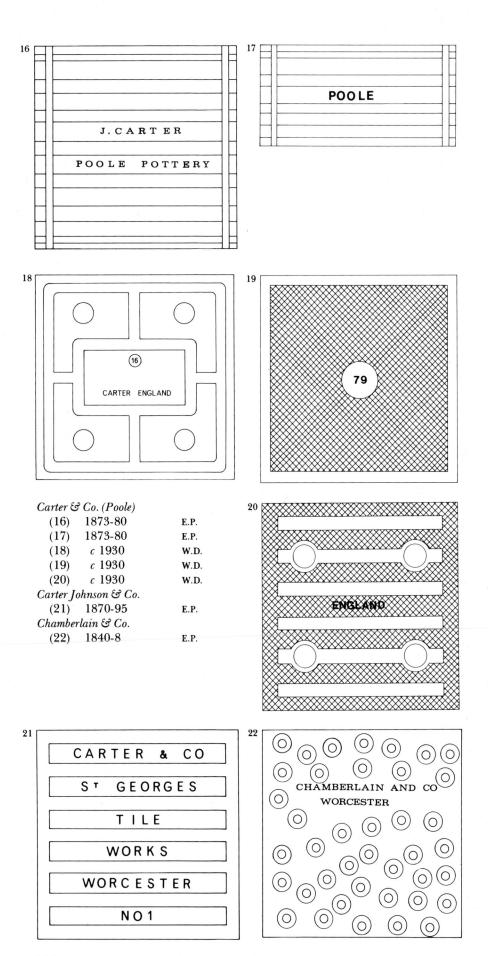

16 J. CARTER

POOLE POTTERY

17 POOLE

18 CARTER ENGLAND

19 79

Carter & Co. (Poole)
(16) 1873-80   E.P.
(17) 1873-80   E.P.
(18) c 1930   W.D.
(19) c 1930   W.D.
(20) c 1930   W.D.
Carter Johnson & Co.
(21) 1870-95   E.P.
Chamberlain & Co.
(22) 1840-8   E.P.

20 ENGLAND

21 CARTER & CO

Sᵀ GEORGES

TILE

WORKS

WORCESTER

NO 1

22 CHAMBERLAIN AND CO
WORCESTER

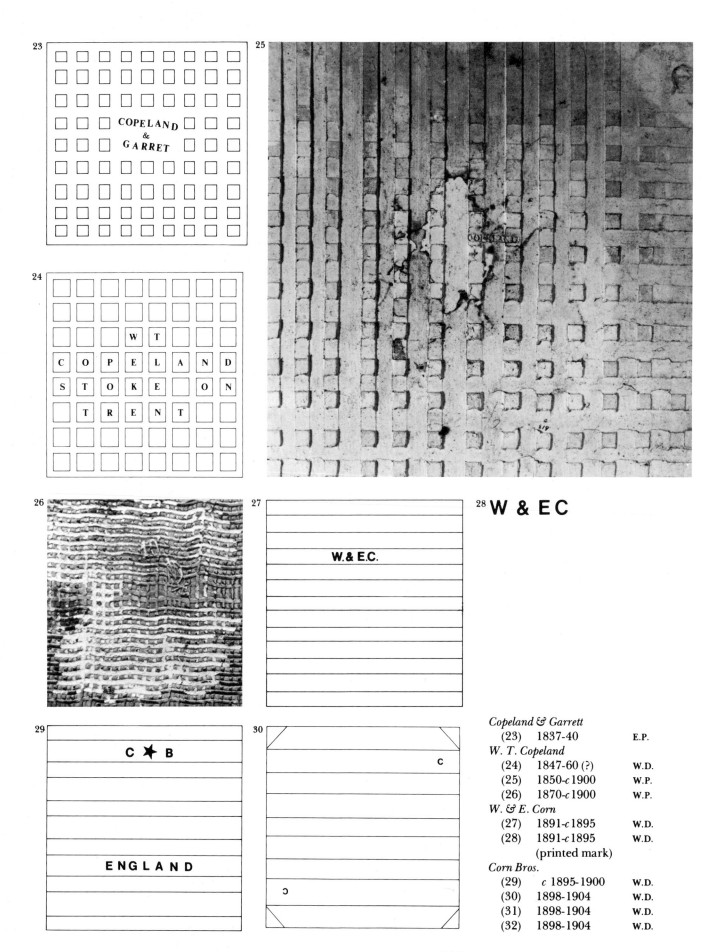

23

COPELAND
&
GARRET

24

W T
C O P E L A N D
S T O K E O N
T R E N T

25

26

27

W.& E.C.

28 W & EC

29

C ★ B

E N G L A N D

30

c

ɔ

Copeland & Garrett
   (23)   1837-40   E.P.
W. T. Copeland
   (24)   1847-60 (?)   W.D.
   (25)   1850-*c*1900   W.P.
   (26)   1870-*c*1900   W.P.
W. & E. Corn
   (27)   1891-*c*1895   W.D.
   (28)   1891-*c*1895   W.D.
         (printed mark)
Corn Bros.
   (29)   *c* 1895-1900   W.D.
   (30)   1898-1904   W.D.
   (31)   1898-1904   W.D.
   (32)   1898-1904   W.D.

Craven Dunnill & Co.

(33)	1871-c1900	W.D.
(34)	1871-c1910	W.D.
(35)	1871-c1910	W.D.
(36)	c1880-c1910	W.D.
(37)	c1880-c1900	W.D.
(38)	1871-c1910	W.D.
(39)	1880-c1910	W.P.
(40)	1900-c1910	W.P.D.
(41)	c1910-1920	W.D.

31
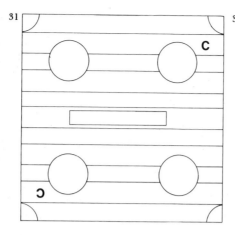

32
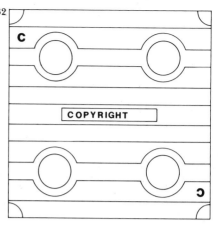

33
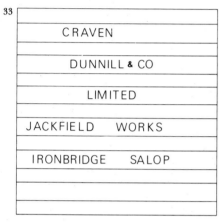

34
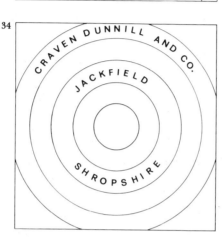

35
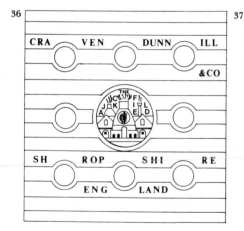

36

37
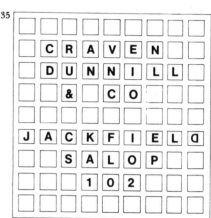

38

39
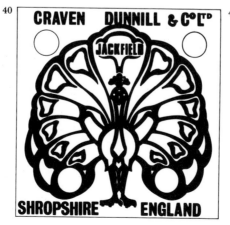

40

41
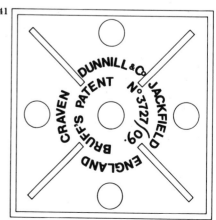

133

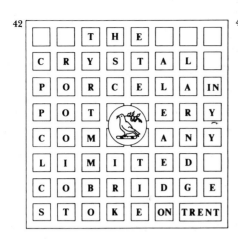

42

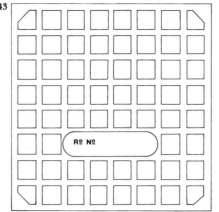

43

44

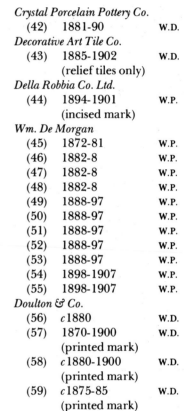

45

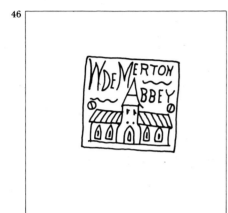

46

W DE MORGAN

47

48

49

50

51

52

WM DE
MORGAN
AND CO
SANDS
END
POTTERY
FVLHAM
S.W.

53

DM
98

54

55

DOULTON
LAMBETH

57

58

Crystal Porcelain Pottery Co.
  (42)   1881-90   W.D.
Decorative Art Tile Co.
  (43)   1885-1902   W.D.
           (relief tiles only)
Della Robbia Co. Ltd.
  (44)   1894-1901   W.P.
           (incised mark)
Wm. De Morgan
  (45)   1872-81   W.P.
  (46)   1882-8   W.P.
  (47)   1882-8   W.P.
  (48)   1882-8   W.P.
  (49)   1888-97   W.P.
  (50)   1888-97   W.P.
  (51)   1888-97   W.P.
  (52)   1888-97   W.P.
  (53)   1888-97   W.P.
  (54)   1898-1907   W.P.
  (55)   1898-1907   W.P.
Doulton & Co.
  (56)   c1880   W.D.
  (57)   1870-1900   W.D.
           (printed mark)
  (58)   c1880-1900   W.D.
           (printed mark)
  (59)   c1875-85   W.D.
           (printed mark)

56

59

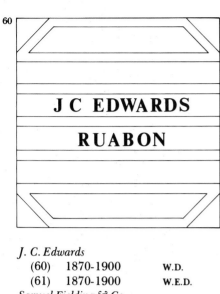

60

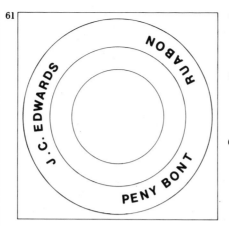

61

J C EDWARDS
RUABON

J. C. EDWARDS
RUABON
PENY BONT

62 **S.F & Co.**

65 **W<u>m</u> GODWIN**
LUGWARDINE

69 **G&H.H**

J. C. Edwards
  (60)   1870-1900   W.D.
  (61)   1870-1900   W.E.D.
Samuel Fielding & Co.
  (62)   1880-90   W.D.
        (printed mark)
Gibbons Hinton
  (63)   1895-1910   W.D.
Wm. Godwin
  (64)   1851-1900   W.D. &
                            D.P.E.
  (65)   1851-63   P.E.
  (66)   1851-1900   P.E.
  (67)   *c*1880-1900   W.D.
Godwin & Hewitt
  (68)   1882-*c*1900   W.D.
        (England after
        1891)
  (69)   1889-1909   W.D. & P.E.
        (printed &
        impressed)
H. & R. Johnson
  (70)   1901-10   W.D.
  (71)   *c*1930   W.D.

63

64

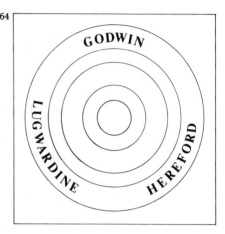

GODWIN
LUGWARDINE
HEREFORD

66

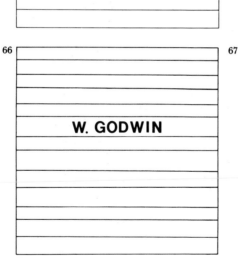

W. GODWIN

67

GODWINS
GODWIN TILE
TRADE MARK

68

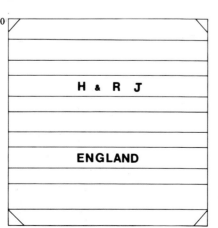

ENGLAND
RD Nº
ENGLAND

70

H & R J
ENGLAND

71

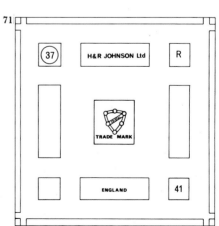

37   H&R JOHNSON Ltd   R
TRADE MARK
ENGLAND   41

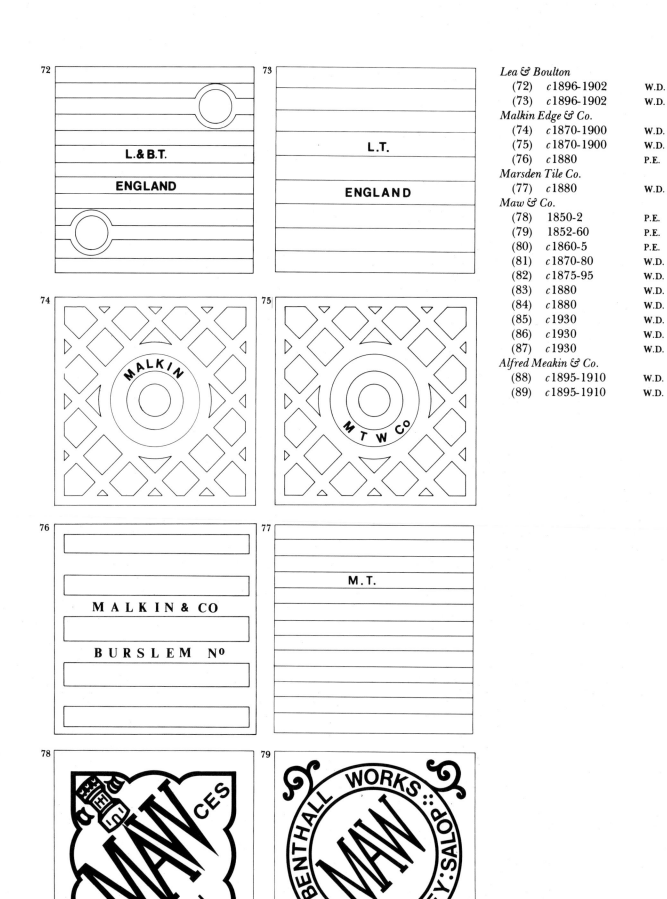

72 L.& B.T. ENGLAND

73 L.T. ENGLAND

74 MALKIN

75 M T W Cᵒ

76 MALKIN & CO BURSLEM Nᵒ

77 M.T.

78 MAW WORCESTER

79 BENTHALL WORKS MAW NR BROSELEY · SALOP

Lea & Boulton
(72)	*c*1896-1902	W.D.
(73)	*c*1896-1902	W.D.

Malkin Edge & Co.
(74)	*c*1870-1900	W.D.
(75)	*c*1870-1900	W.D.
(76)	*c*1880	P.E.

Marsden Tile Co.
(77)	*c*1880	W.D.

Maw & Co.
(78)	1850-2	P.E.
(79)	1852-60	P.E.
(80)	*c*1860-5	P.E.
(81)	*c*1870-80	W.D.
(82)	*c*1875-95	W.D.
(83)	*c*1880	W.D.
(84)	*c*1880	W.D.
(85)	*c*1930	W.D.
(86)	*c*1930	W.D.
(87)	*c*1930	W.D.

Alfred Meakin & Co.
(88)	*c*1895-1910	W.D.
(89)	*c*1895-1910	W.D.

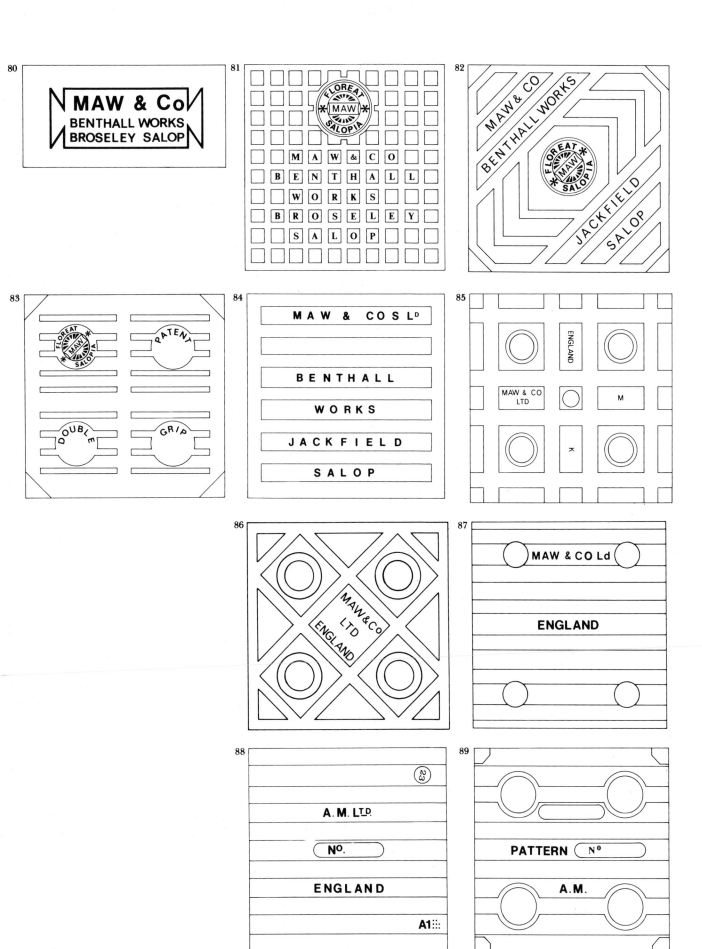

90

91
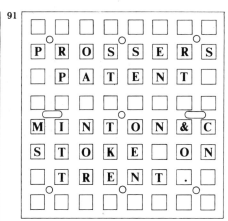

92
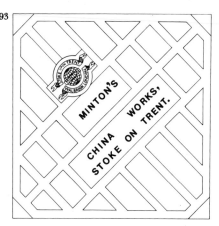

MINTONS

CHINA WORKS

STOKE ON TRENT

93
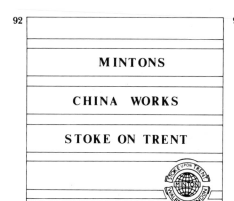

94
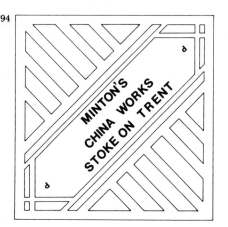

95
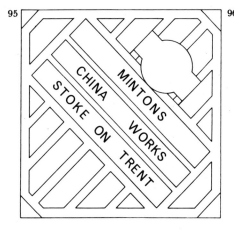

96
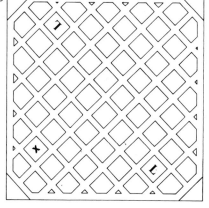

97
MINTONS

CHINA   WORKS

STOKE   ON   TRENT

ENGLAND

138

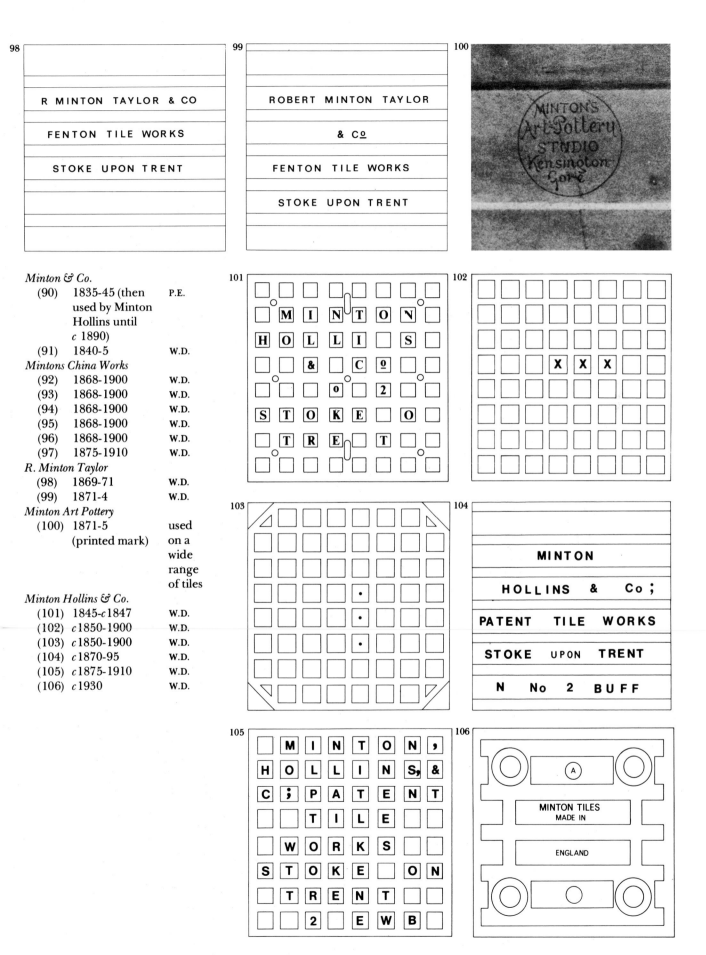

98 R MINTON TAYLOR & CO / FENTON TILE WORKS / STOKE UPON TRENT

99 ROBERT MINTON TAYLOR / & Cᵒ / FENTON TILE WORKS / STOKE UPON TRENT

100 MINTONS Art Pottery STUDIO Kensington Gore

Minton & Co.

(90) 1835-45 (then used by Minton Hollins until c 1890) P.E.

(91) 1840-5 W.D.

Mintons China Works

(92) 1868-1900 W.D.
(93) 1868-1900 W.D.
(94) 1868-1900 W.D.
(95) 1868-1900 W.D.
(96) 1868-1900 W.D.
(97) 1875-1910 W.D.

R. Minton Taylor

(98) 1869-71 W.D.
(99) 1871-4 W.D.

Minton Art Pottery

(100) 1871-5 (printed mark) used on a wide range of tiles

Minton Hollins & Co.

(101) 1845-c1847 W.D.
(102) c1850-1900 W.D.
(103) c1850-1900 W.D.
(104) c1870-95 W.D.
(105) c1875-1910 W.D.
(106) c1930 W.D.

104 MINTON / HOLLINS & Cᵒ; / PATENT TILE WORKS / STOKE UPON TRENT / N No 2 BUFF

105 MINTON, HOLLINS, & C; PATENT TILE WORKS STOKE ON TRENT 2 EWB

106 MINTON TILES MADE IN ENGLAND

139

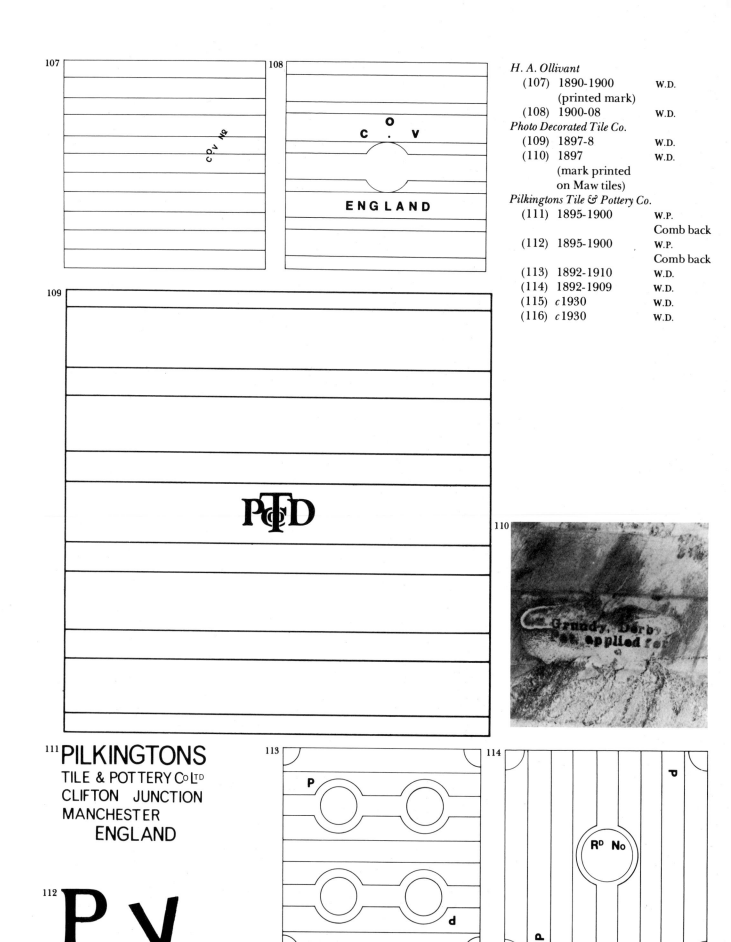

107 — C P V N2

108 — C O V · ENGLAND

109 — PTCD

110 — Grundy, Derby Pat applied for

111 — PILKINGTONS TILE & POTTERY Co LTD CLIFTON JUNCTION MANCHESTER ENGLAND

112 — P V

113 — P d

114 — P RD No P

H. A. Ollivant
(107) 1890-1900   W.D.
     (printed mark)
(108) 1900-08   W.D.
Photo Decorated Tile Co.
(109) 1897-8   W.D.
(110) 1897   W.D.
     (mark printed
     on Maw tiles)
Pilkingtons Tile & Pottery Co.
(111) 1895-1900   W.P.
     Comb back
(112) 1895-1900   W.P.
     Comb back
(113) 1892-1910   W.D.
(114) 1892-1909   W.D.
(115) *c*1930   W.D.
(116) *c*1930   W.D.

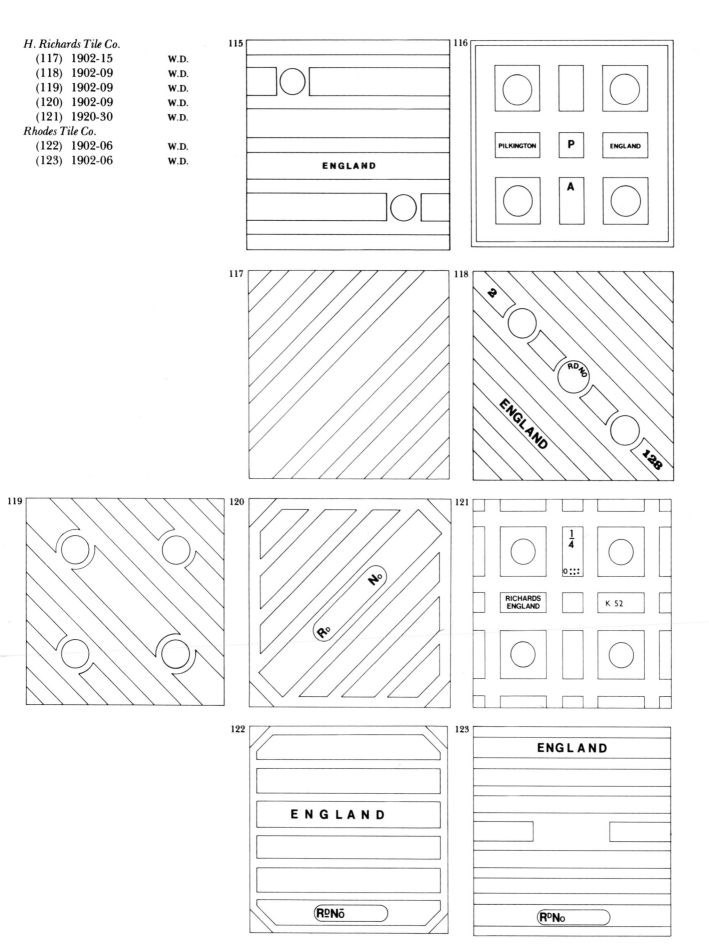

H. Richards Tile Co.
(117) 1902-15   W.D.
(118) 1902-09   W.D.
(119) 1902-09   W.D.
(120) 1902-09   W.D.
(121) 1920-30   W.D.
Rhodes Tile Co.
(122) 1902-06   W.D.
(123) 1902-06   W.D.

115

ENGLAND

116

PILKINGTON   P   ENGLAND

A

117

118

2

RD NO

ENGLAND

128

119

120

No

RD

121

1/4

0 :::

RICHARDS
ENGLAND

K 52

122

ENGLAND

RD NO

123

ENGLAND

RD NO

141

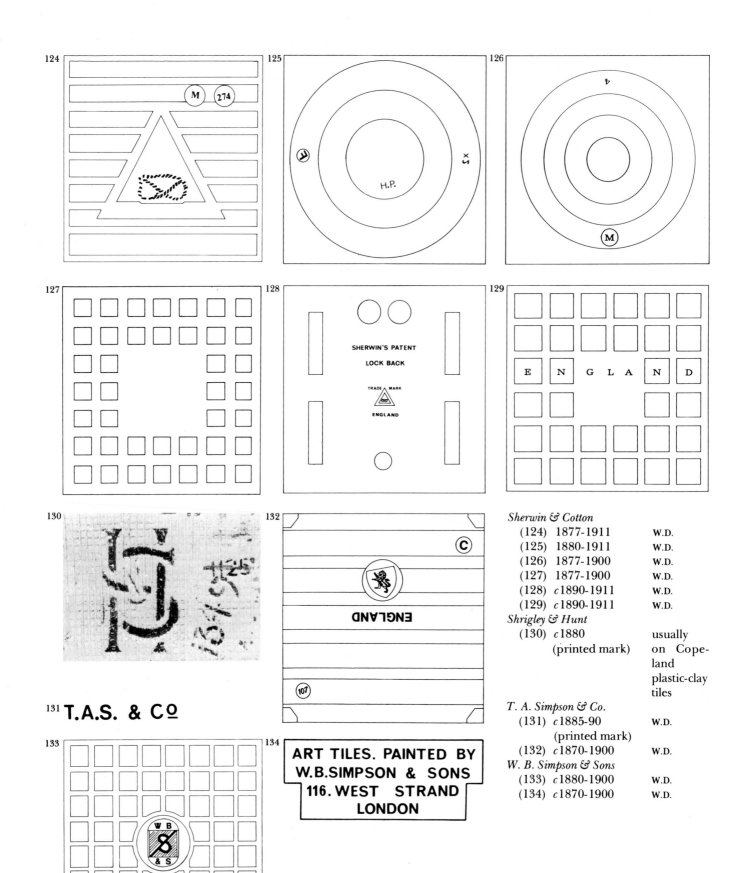

124

125

126

127

128

SHERWIN'S PATENT

LOCK BACK

TRADE MARK

ENGLAND

129

E N G L A N D

130

131 **T.A.S. & Cᴼ**

132

ENGLAND

107

133

134

ART TILES. PAINTED BY
W.B.SIMPSON & SONS
116. WEST STRAND
LONDON

Sherwin & Cotton
(124) 1877-1911   W.D.
(125) 1880-1911   W.D.
(126) 1877-1900   W.D.
(127) 1877-1900   W.D.
(128) *c*1890-1911   W.D.
(129) *c*1890-1911   W.D.
Shrigley & Hunt
(130) *c*1880   usually
(printed mark)   on Copeland
   plastic-clay
   tiles

T. A. Simpson & Co.
(131) *c*1885-90   W.D.
(printed mark)
(132) *c*1870-1900   W.D.
W. B. Simpson & Sons
(133) *c*1880-1900   W.D.
(134) *c*1870-1900   W.D.

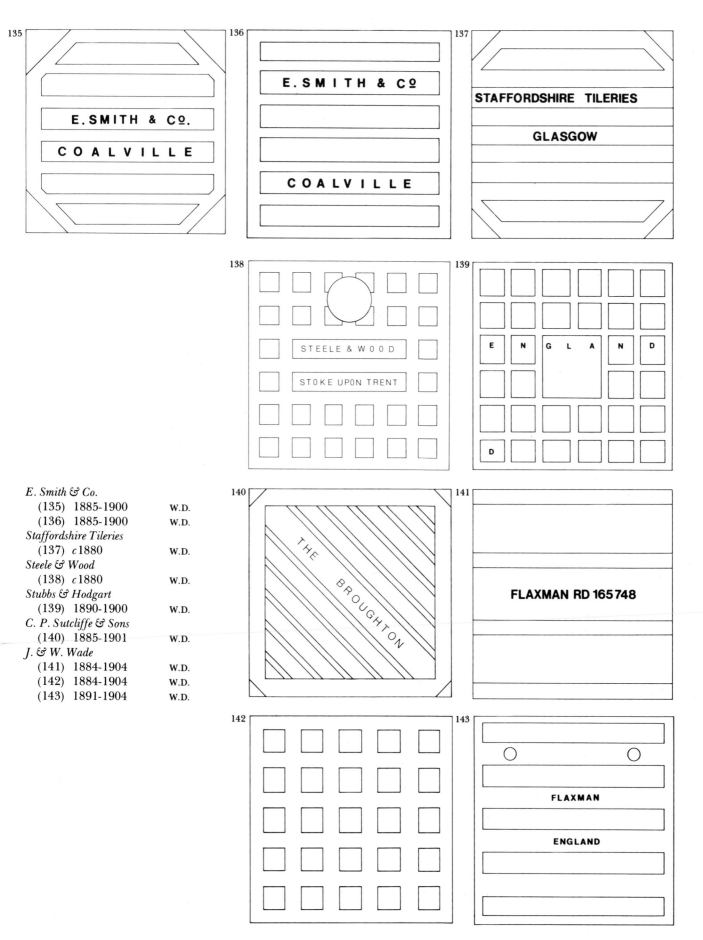

135 E. SMITH & CO. COALVILLE

136 E. SMITH & CO COALVILLE

137 STAFFORDSHIRE TILERIES GLASGOW

138 STEELE & WOOD STOKE UPON TRENT

139 E N G L A N D D

140 THE BROUGHTON

141 FLAXMAN RD 165748

142

143 FLAXMAN ENGLAND

E. Smith & Co.
  (135) 1885-1900   W.D.
  (136) 1885-1900   W.D.
Staffordshire Tileries
  (137) c1880   W.D.
Steele & Wood
  (138) c1880   W.D.
Stubbs & Hodgart
  (139) 1890-1900   W.D.
C. P. Sutcliffe & Sons
  (140) 1885-1901   W.D.
J. & W. Wade
  (141) 1884-1904   W.D.
  (142) 1884-1904   W.D.
  (143) 1891-1904   W.D.

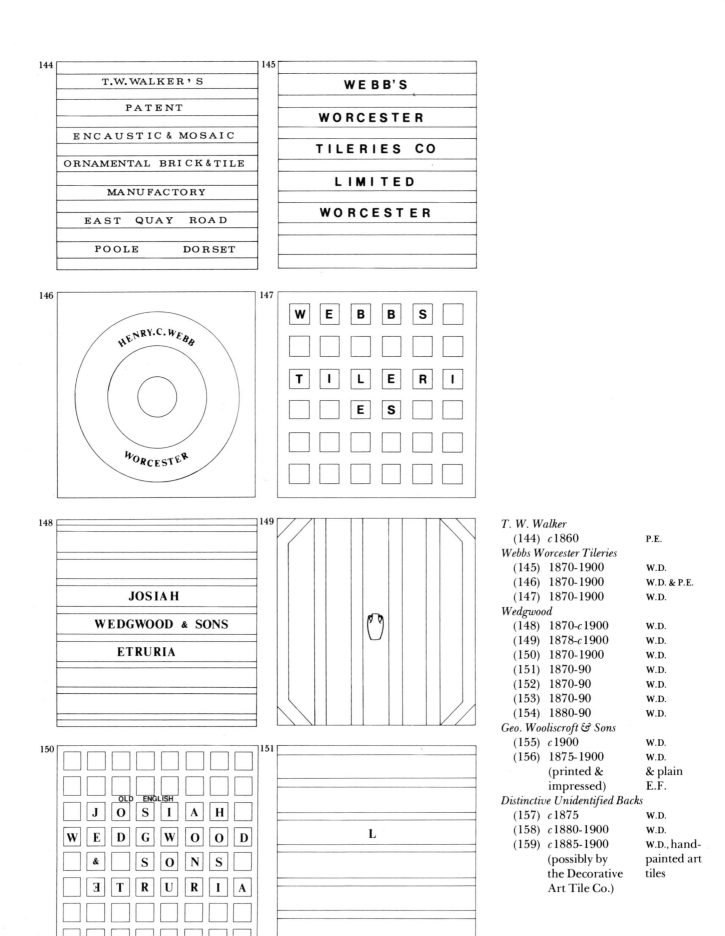

144 T.W.WALKER'S PATENT ENCAUSTIC & MOSAIC ORNAMENTAL BRICK & TILE MANUFACTORY EAST QUAY ROAD POOLE DORSET

145 WEBB'S WORCESTER TILERIES CO LIMITED WORCESTER

146 HENRY.C.WEBB WORCESTER

147 WEBBS TILERIES

148 JOSIAH WEDGWOOD & SONS ETRURIA

149

150 OLD ENGLISH JOSIAH WEDGWOOD & SONS ETRURIA

151 L

T. W. Walker
   (144) *c*1860   P.E.
Webbs Worcester Tileries
   (145) 1870-1900   W.D.
   (146) 1870-1900   W.D. & P.E.
   (147) 1870-1900   W.D.
Wedgwood
   (148) 1870-*c*1900 W.D.
   (149) 1878-*c*1900 W.D.
   (150) 1870-1900   W.D.
   (151) 1870-90   W.D.
   (152) 1870-90   W.D.
   (153) 1870-90   W.D.
   (154) 1880-90   W.D.
Geo. Wooliscroft & Sons
   (155) *c*1900   W.D.
   (156) 1875-1900   W.D.
        (printed &   & plain
        impressed)   E.F.
Distinctive Unidentified Backs
   (157) *c*1875   W.D.
   (158) *c*1880-1900 W.D.
   (159) *c*1885-1900 W.D., hand-
        (possibly by   painted art
        the Decorative tiles
        Art Tile Co.)

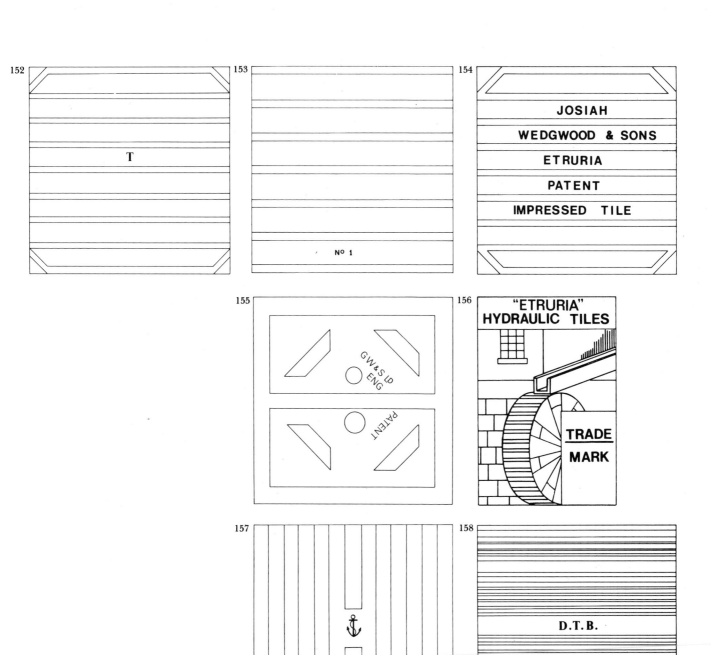

152
T

153
№ 1

154
JOSIAH
WEDGWOOD & SONS
ETRURIA
PATENT
IMPRESSED TILE

155
GW&S LD
ENG
PATENT

156
"ETRURIA"
HYDRAULIC TILES
TRADE
MARK

157

158
D.T.B.

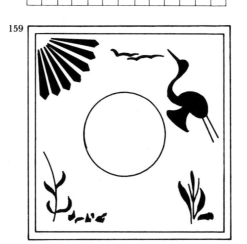

159

APPENDIX B

Popular Picture Tile Series

The following lists of picture tiles produced by various manufacturers has been compiled by assimilating information from factory archives, pattern books, catalogues, design registration records, museums, libraries, contemporary publications and press cuttings, information supplied by dealers and collectors, and our own records.

The dates given refer to the probable introduction of the tile to the manufacturer's range and one must remember that tiles were introduced, withdrawn and reintroduced as fashions changed, and that a tile design drawn in one year, need not necessarily appear on the actual tile for a number of years. Similarly, a tile design may not appear in the pattern book in the correct chronological sequence. Bearing these points in mind, and combining them with a study of the actual tiles over a number of years, we hope we have been able to steer a path through the tangled web of sometimes conflicting evidence. So far as the designers are concerned, very few of their designs are actually signed; attribution has to be based on similarities between the tile and design and other similar work, and knowledge of for whom the artist was working at the time.

Where possible we have kept to the original spelling and punctuation of the series and tile names which appear either on the tiles themselves or in company catalogues and other related literature. Unfortunately, some of the series are incomplete, a few pattern numbers are untraceable, and factories for whom there are no records have been omitted altogether; their picture tiles remain anonymous. We would be extremely pleased to hear from anyone having any information regarding the "missing" tiles so that we may complete the lists for future editions.

To save space, tile measurements are given in inches only. The metric equivalents are as follows: 4 in = 10 cm; 5 in = 13 cm; 6 in = 15 cm; 8 in = 20 cm; and 12 in = 30 cm.

*Mintons China Works
Picture Tile Series*

Pattern No. 12: Watteau Subjects (see page 50). Introduced in limited numbers *c* 1848, though most commonly found on tiles dating from the 1870s. 12 printed pictures on 6 in × 6 in tiles (blue, black, brown): (a) *Children making necklaces.* (b) *Three children playing on see-saw.* (c) *Boy talking to girl with hoe.* (d) *Three children feeding hens.* (e) *Two children and mother resting by a river.* (f) *Two children sitting on a bank.* (g) *Man playing violin to two girls.* (h) *Girl standing by pedestal handing flowers to boy and girl.* (i) *Courting couple under tree.* (j) *Boy playing flute to woman.*

Pattern No. 37: Pseudo Delft Landscapes. 4 printed pictures on 6 in × 6 in tiles. Central design enclosed in double circle with corner motifs. Introduced in limited numbers of tiles from 1850s though most commonly found on tiles dating from 1870s.

Pattern No. 57: Rustic Figures. Introduced in limited numbers of tiles from *c* 1855, though most commonly found on tiles dating from 1870. 8 subjects printed on 6 in × 6 in tiles (sepia, blue, black): (a) *Shepherd resting under a tree.* (b) *Boy in a stream.* (c) *Hay raking.* (d) *Girl feeding tame rabbits.* (e) *Boy and girl with puppy.* (f) *Woman and child resting from collecting sticks.* (g) *Seated girl with goat and kid.* (h) *Young woman carrying pail over stream.*

Pattern No. 58: Landscapes. 4 printed pictures on 6 in × 6 in tiles. Vignetted landscape scene within a leaf and berry border. Introduced on limited numbers of tiles from *c* 1855, though most commonly found on tiles dated from the 1870s.

Pattern No. 1335: Old Testament (J. Moyr Smith) *c* 1870. (See page 106). 12 subjects printed on 6 in × 6 in and 8 in × 8 in tiles (brown/white, brown/buff, black, black/buff, blue): (a) *Adam and Eve driven out of Eden.* (b) *Death of Abel.* (c) *Lot's wife.* (d) *Hagar and Ishmael.* (e) *Abraham offering Isaac.* (f) *Jacob's Dream.* (g) *Joseph before King Pharoah.* (h) *Death of the firstborn.* (i) *Finding of Moses.* (j) *Samson slaying the Philistines.* (k) *Eli and Samuel.* (l) *David playing before Saul.*

Pattern No. 1342: Industrial (J. Moyr Smith) *c* 1870. (See page 107.) 12 subjects printed on 6 in × 6 in tiles (black/white, blue/white, brown, coloured): (a) *Smith.* (b) *Painter.* (c) *Tailor.* (d) *Potter.* (e) *Tanner.* (f) *Carpenter.* (g) *Barber.* (h) *Weaver.* (i) *Shoemaker.* (j) *Dyer.* (k) *Mason.* (l) *Plumber.*

Pattern No. 1344: Early English History (J. Moyr Smith)ʹ*c* 1870. 12 subjects printed on 6 in × 6 in tiles (light and dark brown, blue, black): (a) *Landing of the Romans.* (b) *Edy and Elgiva.* (c) *Lilla saving Edwin.* (d) *Calcactus.* (e) *Canute on the sea shore.* (f) *Boadicea.* (g) *Edward the martyr.* (h) *Death of Harold.* (i) *St. Augustine.* (j) *Alfred and the cakes.* (k) *Harold's oath.* (l) *Alfred in the Danish camp.*

Pattern No. 1346: New Testament (J. Moyr Smith) *c* 1871. 12 subjects printed on 6 in × 6 in and 8 in × 8 in tiles (brown, brown/buff, black, black/buff, blue): (a) *Adoration of the wise men.* (b) *Going up to Jerusalem to the feast.* (c) *Christ disputing with the doctors.* (d) *Christ turning water into wine.* (e) *Christ stilling the tempest.* (f) *Christ blessing little children.* (g) *Christ walking on the sea.* (h) *Jairus's daughter.* (i) *The temptation.* (j) *The crucifixion.* (k) *Christ* *mocked by the soldiers.* (l) *Christ appearing to Mary Magdalene.*

Pattern No. 1347: **Spirit of the Flowers** (J. Moyr Smith) *c* 1872-3. (See page 106.) 12 subjects printed on 6 in × 6 in tiles (blues, brown, black): (a) *Snowdrop.* (b) *Waterlily.* (c) *Lily of the Valley.* (d) *Foxglove.* (e) *Daisy.* (f) *Primrose.* (g) *Violet.* (h) *Convolvulus.* (i) *Anemone.* (j) *Poppy.* (k) *Wild Rose.* (l) *Lily.*

Pattern No. 1364: **Fables** (J. Moyr Smith) *c* 1872. (See page 106.) 12 subjects printed on 6 in × 6 in and 8 in × 8 in tiles (brown and buff, black, brown): (a) *The Dog and the Shadow.* (b) *The Fox and the Goat in the Well.* (c) *The Hare and Tortoise.* (d) *King Log and King Stork.* (e) *The Wolf and the Lamb.* (f) *The Fox and the Crow.* (g) *The Tortoise and the Eagle.* (h) *The Fox and the Stork.* (i) *The Lion and the Mouse.* (j) *The Wolf and the Crane.* (k) *The Monkey and the Cat.* (l) *The Goat, Sheep, and the Calf in Partnership with the Lion.*

Pattern No. 1366: **Fairy Tales** (J. Moyr Smith) *c* 1872. 12 subjects printed on 6 in × 6 in tiles (blue, brown and buff, black): (a) *Golden Locks.* (b) *Snowdrop.* (c) *Frog Prince.* (d) *The Sleeping Beauty.* (e) *The Six Swans.* (f) *Cinderella.* (g) *The Little Tailor.* (h) *Jack and the Beanstalk.* (i) *Blue Beard.* (j) *Rumpelstilzchen.* (k) *Puss in Boots.* (l) *Beauty and the Beast.*

Pattern No. 1407: **Husbandry** (J. Moyr Smith) *c* 1873. 12 subjects printed on 6 in × 6 in tiles (browns, brown/buff): (a) *Ploughing.* (b) *Fishing.* (c) *Reaping corn.* (d) *Gathering fruit.* (e) *Reaping.* (f) *Threshing.* (g) *Digging.* (h) *Gardening.*

Pattern No. 1408: **Shakespeare** (J. Moyr Smith) *c* 1873. 24 subjects printed on 6 in × 6 in and 8 in × 8 in tiles (brown, blue, black with yellow border; 18 selected subjects from these also done in tinted grey monochrome, No. 1665; and sepia monochrome, No. 1696): (a) *Romeo and Juliet (I, i).* (b) *Romeo and Juliet (III, ii).* (c) *Macbeth (III, iv).* (d) *Macbeth (V, vii).* (e) *The Tempest (I, ii).* (f) *The Tempest (II, ii).* (g) *Cymbaline (II, ii).* (h) *Hamlet (I, i).* (i) *Anthony and Cleopatra (IV, iv).* (j) *Anthony and Cleopatra (V, ii).* (k) *Winter's Tale (V, iii).* (l) *King Lear (I, i).* (m) *King Lear (V, iii).* (n) *Twelfth Night (II, iii).* (o) *Twelfth Night (III, iv).* (p) *Midsummer Night's Dream (IV, i).* (q) *Troilus and Cressida (IV, ii).* (r) *Merchant of Venice (II, ii).* (s) *Merchant of Venice (IV, i).* (t) *Othello (I, iii).* (u) *Taming of the Shrew (IV, iii).* (v) *Much Ado about Nothing (IV, ii).* (w) *Timon of Athens (III, vi).* (x) *King Henry IV (II, iv).*

Pattern No. 1409: **Water Nymphs** (J. Moyr Smith) *c* 1873. 12 subjects printed on 6 in × 6 in tiles (blue, brown and black): (a) *Water nymphs playing a harp.* (b) *Water nymphs with a fish.*

Pattern No. 1410: **Elfins** *c* 1873. (See page 50.) 12 subjects printed on 6 in × 6 in tiles (blue, brown and buff, and black): (a) *Frog leap-frogging an elfin.* (b) *Elfin leap-frogs a frog.* (c) *Elfin sitting on toadstool.* (d) *Elfin with stag-beetle.* (e) *Elfin with sword fighting lizard.* (f) *Elfin riding a shrew.* (g) *Elfin doffing his hat to a mole.* (h) *Elfin leaping.* (i) *Elfin riding a bat.* (j) *Elfin holding an egg, with two birds anxiously watching.*

Pattern No. 1455: **Rustic Humours** *c* 1875. 12 subjects printed on 6 in × 6 in tiles (blue, brown, black): (a) *Suspicion.* (b) *Ignorance.* (c) *Ambition.* (d) *Idleness.*

Pattern No. 1465: **Idylls of the King** (J. Moyr Smith) *c* 1875. (See page 105.) 12 subjects printed on 6 in × 6 in tiles (dark brown and blue on a buff background, dark brown and blue on a white background, dark brown and buff on an orange background, light brown on white): (a) *The lady of the lake gives the sword to King Arthur.* (b) *Gareth entering the town.* (c) *Gareth and Lynette on their journey, Lynette jeers at Gareth.* (d) *Pelleas first sees Etarre.* (e) *Pelleas finds Gawin and Etarre asleep in the pavilion.* (f) *Enid and Limours.* (g) *Geraint slays Dorm.* (h) *Elaine's body in the barge.* (i) *Vivien puts forth the charm on Merlin.* (j) *Tristram and Isolt.* (k) *King Arthur and Guinevere.* (l) *King Arthur in the barge with the three queens.*

Pattern No. 1501: **Classical Musicians** (J. Moyr Smith) 1876-7. (See page 106.) 8 subjects printed on 6 in × 6 in and 8 in × 8 in (No. 1502) tiles (plain prints and coloured, yellow figure on blue ground enclosed by a brown surround, brown on white background, white figure on blue ground enclosed by yellow surround): (a) *Rotta.* (b) *Cithara.* (c) *Sistrum.* (d) *Celtic harp.* (e) *Tambourine.* (f) *Cymbals.* (g) *Double flute.* (h) *Syrinx* (Pan pipes).

Pattern No. 1607: **Walter Scott's Waverley Novels** (J. Moyr Smith) *c* 1878. (See page 105.) 12 subjects printed on 6 in × 6 in and 8 in × 8 in tiles (yellow-tinted pictures in grey and sepia monochrome on a white background): (a) *Guy Mannering.* (b) *Kenilworth.* (c) *Talisman.* (d) *Rob Roy.* (e) *Bride of Lammermoor.* (f) *Heart of Mid Lothian.* (g) *Fortunes of Nigel.* (h) *Ivanhoe.* (i) *Old Mortality.* (j) *Antiquary.* (k) *Fair Maid of Perth.* (l) *Quentin Durward.*

Anacreon (J. Moyr Smith) *c* 1878. (See page 105.) 12 subjects printed on 8 in × 8 in tiles, also used on tableware (coloured): (a) *Cup bearer.* (b) *The grace.* (c) *The manager.* (d) *The guest.* (e) *The hostess.* (f) *The host.* (g) *The libator.* (h) *The good listener.* (i) *The dessert.* (j) *The master of the revels.*

Pattern No. 1653: **Seven Ages of Birds** 1878-9. 7 subjects printed on 6 in × 6 in tiles (blue/white, black/white).

Pattern No. 1699: **Animals of the Farm** (William Wise) *c* 1879. 12 subjects printed on 6 in × 6 in and 8 in × 8 in tiles (brown on white, brown on buff, blue on white, black on white, polychrome): 6 subjects in the farmyard: (a) *Cart horses.* (b) *Cow in shed.* (c) *Pig at trough.* (d) *Two donkeys.* (e) *Sheep lying down.* (f) *Sheep and lambs by hut.* 6 subjects in the pastures: (g) *Horse and foal under tree.* (h) *Cows in stream.* (i) *Stag and does on pastures.* (j) *Highland sheep.* (k) *Highland cattle.* (l) *Highland goats.*

Pattern No. 1759: **Days of the Week** *c* 1880. (See page 50.) Humorously illustrated in 7 pictures (with an ornamental alternate tile) from drawings by Mrs. E. E. Houghton. These subjects are outlined and tinted by hand in light reds, and also in blues. 6 in × 6 in tiles.

Pattern No. 1762: **Signs of the Zodiac** (H. Stacey Marks) *c* 1880. (See page 101.) Quaintly represented by 12 figure subjects, outlined and painted in colours by hand, on 6 in × 6 in tiles.

Pattern No. 1801: **Village Life** (William Wise) *c* 1882. (See page 109.) 12 subjects printed on 6 in × 6 in tiles (brown/white, black/white, black/buff): (a) *Man carrying scythe.* (b) *Man carrying hoe accompanied by children.* (c) *Woman milking a cow with children nearby.* (d) *Two women and child gleaning corn.* (e) *Shepherd and sheep-dog by a barred gate.* (f) *Woman carrying a child talking to boy.* (g) *Woman and child planting potatoes.* (h) *Woman and child picking bay leaves.*

Pattern No. 1843: **Thompson's Seasons** (J. Moyr Smith) *c* 1882. 12 subjects printed on 6 in × 6 in and 8 in × 8 in tiles (sepia monochrome, grey monochrome, No. 1844): (a) *Spring: emblematical.* (b) *Ploughing.* (c) *The Rainbow.* (d) *Summer: emblematical.* (e) *Celedon and Amelia.* (f) *Musidora and Damon.* (g) *Autumn: emblematical.* (h) *Reaping.* (i) *Lavinia and Palemon.* (j) *Winter: emblematical.* (k) *The Snowstorm.* (l) *Skating.*

Pattern No. 1871: **Gastronomical Series** (J. Moyr Smith) *c* 1882. 12 subjects outlined and painted in colours by hand on 6 in × 6 in tiles. Also done on 8 in × 8 in tiles by the addition of a border (1880): (a) *Chef with saucepan.* (b) *Butler examining a glass of wine in a wine cellar.* (c) *Servant carrying meat on dish.* (d) *Butler removing a soup dish.*

Pattern No. 1895: **Old English Sports and Games** *c* 1882. (See page 52.) 12 pictures outlined and painted in colours by hand on 6 in × 6 in tiles. This series is also hand painted in monochrome: (a) *Hawking.* (b) *Hunting.* (c) *Fishing.* (d) *Coursing.* (e) *Shooting.* (f) *Single combat.* (g) *Skating.* (h) *Croquet.* (i) *Chess playing.* (j) *Football.* (k) *Cricket.* (l) *Rowing.*

Pattern No. 1897: **Fables** (Henk?) *c* 1882. (See page 51.) 12 subjects outlined and painted in monochrome by hand in blues on 6 in × 6 in and 8 in × 8 in tiles (blue on white): (a) *The Lamb and the Wolf.* (b) *The Fox and the Goat in the Well.* (c) *The Hare and the Tortoise.* (d) *King Stork and the Frogs.* (e) *The Lion and the Mouse.* (f) *The Stork Dines with the Fox.* (g) *The Dog and the Bees.* (h) *The Dog and the Cow in the Manger.* (i) *The Boar and the Wolf.* (j) *The Steer and the Frog.* (k) *The Frog, the Mouse and the Hawk.*

Pattern No. 1898: **Scenes in the Hunting Field** *c* 1882. (See page 52.) 12 subjects outlined and tinted in colours by hand on 6 in × 6 in tiles (monochrome, blues or browns): (a) *Keen.* (b) *John.* (c) *Regardless of expense.* (d) *Master's luncheon.* (e) *If women will hunt.* (f) *Arry out hunting.* (g) *Grief over wire.* (h) *A good pilot.* (i) *Heals over head.* (j) *A stern chase.* (k) *Faults on both sides.*

Pattern No. 1899: **Natural History** (Henk ?) *c* 1882. (See page 100.) 12 subjects outlined and painted in colour by hand on 6 in × 6 in tiles: (a) *Owl with foot on mouse.* (b) *Bird and dragonfly.* (c) *Dragonfly and snail.* (d) *Bird and snail.* (e) *Squirrel.* (f) *Two frogs.* (g) *Two rabbits.* (h) *Crab and eel.* (i) *Fish and lobster.* (j) *Butterfly and grasshopper.* (k) *Mouse and acorn.*

Pattern No. 1900: **Shakespeare's Seven Ages of Man** *c* 1882. (See page 101.) From early designs at the Kensington Art Pottery Studio *c* 1873, from drawings by H. S. Marks R. A.: (a) *Infant.* (b) *Schoolboy.* (c) *Lover.* (d) *Soldier.* (e) *Justice.* (f) *The lean and slippered pantaloon.* (g) *Second childhood.* (h) *Youth.* (i) *Age.*

Pattern No. 2017: **Animal Groups** (William Wise) *c* 1883. (See page 109.) 12 subjects, 4 each of horses, cows and sheep, printed in brown outline with grey ground, on 6 in × 6 in tiles. Also done on 8 in × 8 in tiles (No. 2073).

Pattern No. 2024: **Views** (L. T. Swetnam & William Wise) *c* 1885. (See page 49.) 6 in × 6 in and 8 in × 8 in (No. 2029) tiles (brown on white, sepia, coloured, black on white, sepia and white). Confusion surrounds this series since considerably more than 12 views were produced and a full list of them is unavailable. To further complicate matters, the majority of the views are untitled

making a positive identification difficult. The following titles have been recorded: (a) *Conway Castle.* (b) *Boppart on the Rhine.* (c) *Cardinal Beaton's house.* (d) *Dillingen der Donau.* (e) *Village of Splugen.* (f) *Rodez Cathedral.* (g) *West Gate, Warwick.* (h) *The old gate Winchelsea.* (i) *Edinburgh Castle from the Grassmarket.* (j) *Edinburgh Castle* (different view). (k) *Old Edinburgh: The Nether Bow Port from the High Street.* (l) *Inverary Castle.* A further 8 untitled views have also been noted.

Pattern No. 2061: **Sporting** *c* 1886. (See page 46.) 12 subjects printed on 6 in × 6 in tiles (brown outline with grey ground, with buff ground No. 2062): (a) *Shooting.* (b) *Cricket.* (c) *Hawking.* (d) *Hare hunt.* (e) *Fishing.* (f) *Deer stalking.*

Pattern No. 2063: **Birds** (L. T. Swetnam) *c* 1886. 16 subjects printed on 6 in × 6 in and 8 in × 8 in (No. 2079) tiles. 12 of these subjects are coloured by hand in neutral colours (No. 2133).

Pattern No. 2068: **Cooking** (L. M. Solon). (See page 107.) 12 subjects treated humorously. This series sometimes goes under different titles. In blue monochrome on 6 in × 6 in and 8 in × 8 in (No. 2069) tiles. In brown monochrome 6 in × 6 in (No. 2072) and on 8 in × 8 in (No. 2073): (a) *Sausage machine.* (b) *Too many cooks spoil the broth.* (c) *Baron of beef.* (d) *Pigeon pie.* (e) *The last victim.* (f) *Smoked haddocks.* (g) *Hare being caught.* (h) *Fried eels.* (i) *Execution.* (j) *Fish supper.* (k) *Puzzled.* (l) *Fresh eggs.*

Pattern No. 2164: **Country Pursuits** (William Wise) *c* 1886. (See page 109.) 12 subjects printed on 6 in × 6 in and 8 in × 8 in tiles (black/white, brown/cream and hand coloured): (a) *Woman on seashore with small basket of fish.* (b) *Girl feeding poultry and ducks.* (c) *Girl by stream.* (d) *Girl with basket of apples.* (e) *Girl carrying a child in a basket on her back.* (f) *Seated girl with fawns.* (g) *Girl picking berries.* (h) *Girl reading under a tree.*

Pattern No. 2231: **Scenic Views** (L. T. Swetnam) *c* 1890. Series of what appear to be 6 subjects on 6 in × 6 in tiles. Central design in sepia or hand coloured (No. 2251) enclosed within a border: (a) *Alpine lakeside scene.* (b) *Rhineland riverside scene.* (c) *Woman standing in front of thatched cottage.* (d) *Waterfront scene of Flemish fishing boats.* (e) *Windmill on the water front.*

Pattern No. 2455: **Arts and Sciences** (J. Moyr Smith) *c* 1890. 12 subjects outlined and painted in monochrome by hand: (a) *Sculpture.* (b) *Architecture.* (c) *Geology.* (d) *Astronomy.* (e) *Agriculture.* (f) *Mechanics.*

Wedgwood Picture Tiles (1870-1900)

Pattern No. 228: **Chaucer Subject.** Only one design illustrated in the pattern book, probably a series of 6.

Pattern No. 236: **Shepherd of Israel.** Only one design illustrated in the pattern book.

Religious Series: (a) *A saviour Christ the Lord.* (b) *Wise men came to worship.* (c) *They presenteth Him to the Lord.* (d) *Herod seeks to destroy Him.* (e) *They found Him in the Temple.* (f) *The carpenter of Nazareth.* (g) *This is My beloved Son.* (h) *He heals the sick.* (i) *He blesses the children.* (j) *He feeds the multitude.* (k) *He purges His Father's house.* (l) *He raises the dead to live.* (m) *He walks on the sea.* (n) *Hosanna to the Son of David.* (o) *Judas betrayed Him with a kiss.* (p) *He suffered under Pontius Pilate.* (q) *He was crucified dead and buried.* (r) *He rose again from the dead.* (s) *He ascended into heaven.* (t) *Angels came and ministered unto Him.*

Pattern No. 241 (also done on Pattern No. 317 with a border): **Infant Neptune.** (See page 67.) Series of 6 tiles of a water baby playing with deep-sea fish and crustacia (brown on white, blue on white): (a) *Infant Neptune and lobster.* (b) *Infant Neptune riding a fish.* (c) *Infant Neptune playing a shell to an audience of fish.* (d) *Infant Neptune with three fish.* (e) *Infant Neptune giving a fish medicine from a bottle.* (f) *Infant Neptune and three lobsters.*

Pattern No. 269: **Ye Army/Ye Church.** Printed on 6 in × 6 in tiles (blue on white, brown on white).

Pattern No. 270: **Ye Law/Medicine.** Printed on 6 in × 6 in tiles (blue on white, brown on white).

Pattern No. 273: **Where the Carcase Is, There Will the Eagles Be Gathered Together** (T. Allen).

Pattern No. 274: **Fresco Heads.** 5 subjects printed on 6 in × 6 in tiles (brown on white). (a) *Dog.* (b) *Fox.* (c) *Tiger.* (d) *Ram.* (e) *Bull.*

Pattern No. 275: **Months of the Year** (Old English). (See page 65.) 12 subjects printed on 6 in × 6 in and 8 in × 8 in tiles with a border (blue on white, brown on white, black on white, coloured): Children dressed in period costume.

Pattern No. 276: **Red Riding Hood** (Walter Crane?). (See page 66.) 6 subjects printed on 6 in × 6 in tiles, illustrating the story of Little Red Riding Hood (black on white, brown on white, blue on white).

148

Pattern No. 277: **Courses of a Meal** (T. Allen). (See page 95.) 5 subjects printed on 6 in × 6 in tiles (black on white, blue on white): (a) *Soup.* (b) *Fish.* (c) *Venison.* (d) *Mutton.* (e) *Pastry.*

Pattern No. 278: **Midsummer Night's Dream** (T. Allen). (See page 94.) 12 subjects printed on 6 in × 6 in and 8 in × 8 in tiles with a border (brown on white, brown on white): (a) *Bottom.* (b) *Mustard* (sic). (c) *Titania.* (d) *Oberon.* (e) *Peas Blossom.* (f) *Puck.* (g) *Moth.* (h) *Hermia.* (i) *Cobweb.* (j) *Helena.* (k) *Demetrius.* (l) *Lysander.*

Pattern No. 283: **Dogs' Heads.** (See page 67.) 6 subjects printed on 6 in × 6 in and 8 in × 8 in tiles; also found on tableware (brown on white, blue on white).

Pattern No. 285: **Japanese Series.** 12 subjects printed on 6 in × 6 in tiles illustrating orientals at work and play (brown on white).

Pattern No. 286: **Reindeer.** 2 subjects printed on 6 in × 6 in tiles.

Pattern No. 288: **An Eventful Day's Fishing.** 6 subjects printed on 6 in × 6 in tiles; also found on tableware (blue on white, coloured): (a) *Fly fishing* (fisherman catches hat). (b) *Think I shall have a rise here* (bull charging fisherman). (c) *Jolly fisherman* (fisherman under umbrella). (d) *A nibble* (fisherman watching milkmaid). (e) *In a fix* (fisherman with line tangled in branches). (f) *Those horrid boys* (fisherman watching swimming party).

Pattern No. 289: **Homilies.** 12 subjects printed on 6 in × 6 in tiles. Rectangular picture contained within a circular frame captioned round the circumference (brown on white, blue on white, black on white): (a) *By doing nothing we learn to do ill.* (b) *He laughs at scars that never felt a wound.* (c) *The day a man wishes to go thither his feet will carry him.* (d) *Lowliness is young ambition's ladder.* (e) *Treason is not owned when tis discried.* (f) *He that would eat the kernel must crack the nut.* (g) *We lessen our wants by lessening our desires.* (h) *Even the ripest fruit does not drop into one's mouth.* (i) *The circles of our felicities make short arches.* (j) *You must be content sometimes with rough roads.* (k) *Fly the pleasure that bites tomorrow.* (l) *Let another man's shipwreck be your seamark.*

Pattern No. 290: **Scenes in the Hunting Fields.** 6 subjects printed on 6 in × 6 in tiles (brown on white): (a) *Tally Ho.* (b) *Master of the hounds.* (c) *A good shot.* (d) *Stand back* (stag at bay). (e) *1st October* (man shooting). (f) *1st September* (hunter and 2 retrievers).

Pattern No. 291: **Game Series.** (See page 67.) 6 subjects printed on 8 in × 8 in tiles (black on white, blue on white): (a) *Hare running.* (b) *Nesting grouse.* (c) *Surprised dog and grouse.* (d) *Gun dog and dead game.* (e) *Snipe and eggs.* (f) *Two pheasants.*

Pattern No. 292: **Classical Musicians in an Orange Grove** (Walter Crane?). (See page 67.) 6 subjects painted on 6 in × 6 in tiles (blue on white, black on white, brown on cream): (a) *A seated man and standing woman playing recorder.* (b) *Woman playing tambourine.* (c) *Woman playing zither.* (d) *Seated man playing violin to a woman.* (e) *Man playing pipes of Pan to woman.* (f) *Man playing cithara to woman.*

Pattern No. 329: **Hats** (T. Allen). (See page 95.) 7 subjects printed on 6 in × 6 in and 8 in × 8 in tiles with various borders. Each illustrating a child in a different hat (blue on white, black on white, brown on white).

Pattern No. 335: **Ivanhoe** (T. Allen). (See page 95.) 10 subjects printed on 8 in × 8 in tiles (brown on cream, blue on white); also found on tableware (a) *The Black Knight exchanges buffets with Friar Tuck.* (b) *Rowena granting a safe escort to Rebecca and her father.* (c) *Front de Boeuf extorting silver from Isaac the Jew.* (d) *Rebecca repelling the Templar.* (e) *Ivanhoe and Rowena.* (f) *Wambo and Gurtherd the swineherd.* (g) *Rebecca gives a purse of money to Garth.*

Pattern No. 357: **Children's Pastimes.** 6 subjects printed on 6 in × 6 in tiles (brown on white): (a) *Two children and a calf.* (b) *Boy throwing frog in air.* (c) *Boy and girl with bird's nest.* (d) *Boy and girl with lamb.* (e) *Boy and girl playing with shuttlecock.* (f) *Boy and girl fishing.*

Pattern No. 427: **Series of Game Birds.** 12 subjects printed on 6 in × 6 in tiles (brown on white): (a) *Geese.* (b) *Turkey.* (c) *Quail.* (d) *Cockerel, hen and chicken.* (e) *Ptarmigan.* (f) *Grouse.* (g) *Cockerel.* (h) *Two pheasants.* (i) *Rabbits.* (j) *Moorhen.* (k) *Fox.* (l) *Pigeons.*

Pattern No. 432: **Sea Shells.** 12 subjects printed on 8 in × 8 in tiles illustrating various sea shells (brown on white).

Pattern Nos. 575, 576, 577: **Authors.** Series of 3 authors on 6 in × 6 in tiles. Portraits contained in an oval border of oak leaves and acorns. Other portraits are also known on tiles with this border, e.g., Edward VII (brown on white): (575) *Swinburne.* (576) *Dickens.* (577) *Shakespeare.*

American Series. This series can be found in brown, and blue. Pattern numbers: (294) *National Capital, Washington.* (295) *Washington Statue, public gardens, Boston.* (296) *Bunkers Hill monument.* (297) *Summer Statue, public gardens, Boston.* (298) *Trinity Church, Boston.* (299) *Commonwealth Avenue.* (300) *Public gardens, Boston.* (301) *Old South Church, Boston.* (302) *Niagara falls — Prospect Point.* (417) *Landing of the pilgrims, 1620.* (418) *Old Hume.* (419) *The Maplewood White Mountain, New Hampshire.* (420) *New Hume.* (421) *Nantasket House, Nantasket Beacon.* (422) *Unidentified.* (423) *Beacon St., Boston.* (424) *Unidentified.* (426) *Maplewood House.* (430) *Hotel Pemberton, Hull, Mass.* (486) *The Boston common.* (487) *Boston monument.* (488) *Museum of fine arts.* (489) *Grey St. and Theatre Royal.* (493) *Sailing ship* — Intrepid. (494) *The Lillie of Telegraph Hill.* (497) *The Rebecca.* (498) *St. Nicholas Cathedral.* (499) *St. Mary's Catholic Church.* (500) *High-level and swing bridges.* (501) *Arlington St., Boston.* (502) *Institute of Technology, Boston.* (503) *Chauncy Hall School, Boston.*

Calendar tiles were produced annually for "Jones McDuffee & Stratton, Boston". They were given to clients from 1881-1929.

Copeland Tiles

Months of the Year — Women in Classical Dress *c* 1855. (See page 58.) 6 subjects on hand-painted 6 in × 6 in tiles. 2 figures on each tile, representative of the month's occupation in classical-style dress.

The Four Seasons and Father Time. 1875. 5 subjects on 6 in × 6 in tiles. A central portrait contained within 4 adjoining circles within which are illustrated the flora and fauna associated with the season (blue monochrome): (a) *Spring.* (b) *Summer.* (c) *Autumn.* (d) *Winter.* (e) *Time.*

Months of the Year — Renaissance Style (Lucien Besche) 1875-1880. (See page 56.) 12 subjects on 6 in × 6 in and 8 in × 8 in tiles (cobalt blue monochrome, gold on a red background, cane body, buff, printed and painted in brown): (a) *January.* (b) *February* (man digging). (c) *March* (man holding hat). (d) *April* (woman fishing). (e) *May* (woman feeding fowl). (f) *June* (woman tying up rose tree). (g) *July* (woman with a bundle of wheat). (h) *August* (woman carrying a basket of fruit). (i) *September* (man with dog and hunting horn). (j) *October* (woman squeezing grapes into cup). (k) *November* (man sowing seeds). (l) *December* (man skating).

Months of the Year — with Astrological Symbol 1875-80. 12 subjects on 6 in × 6 in tiles. Design framed within a circle, the month written across the top corners and the astrological name across the bottom corners. 5 subjects so far recorded. (coloured and blue monochrome): (a) *May/Gemini* (woman carrying bunch of flowers). (b) *June/Cancer* (woman holding lamb, and sheep shearers). (c) *July/Leo* (woman raking hay). (d) *August/Virgo* (woman with sickle and bundle of corn). (e) *November/Sagittarius* (male hooper splitting logs with female hooper in background).

Incidents from the Legend of Robin Hood. (See page 57) 25 subjects on 6 in × 6 in tiles each contained within a circle bordered by thistles (coloured): (a) *Robyn Hood & ye Abbot.* (b) *Robyn Hood as a butcher.* (c) *Robyn Hood's last shot.* (d) *Robyn Hood and tinker.* (e) *Robyn Hood and ye beggar.* (f) *Robyn Hood and ye tanner.* (g) *Robyn Hood and ye French pirate.* (h) *Robyn defeats and kills sheriff.* (i) *Robyn Hood and ye abbot.* (j) *Robyn Hood as a potter dines with the sheriff.* (k) *Robyn Hood and ye curtal friar.* (l) *Robyn Hood and Lyttle John.* (m) *Robyn Hood slays Guy of Gisborne.* (n) *Robyn's visit to Squire Gamwel.* (o) *Lyttle John gives ye poore knight good measure.* (p) *Lyttle John and the IV beggars.* (q) *Lyttle John decoys sheriff.* (r) *Lyttle John prisoner.* (s) *Lyttle John and ye sheriff cook.* (t) *Lyttle John wounded and saved by much.* (u) *Lyttle John's baptism.* (v) *The King reveals hymself.* (w) *Syr Richd's ladye askes Robyn Hood to rescue her husband.* (x) *The poore knight asketh for more time.* (y) *Ye poore knight's story.*

Gnomes and Elves *c* 1885. 12 subjects on 6 in × 6 in tiles (cane body with a brown print; celadon body with brown print tinted in blue; celadon body with coloured print): (a) *Music* (gnome conducting frog and sparrow). (b) *Surprise* (gnome discovers a snail under a toadstool). (c) *Ambush* (gnome attacking a bee in a flower). (d) *Rest* (gnome drinking from a harebell). (e) *Message* (tit gives message to the gnome). (f) *Alarm* (gnome is surprised by a bullfrog). (g) *Caught* (elf caught in a spider's web). (h & i) *Til-Ting* (2 tiles: pair of elves tilting, seated on mice, Ting being unseated). (j) *A Prize* (gnome carrying a rat over his shoulder on a stick). (k) *Harvest* (gnome plucking ears of wheat).

Shakespeare Series *c* 1880. (See page 57.) 24 subjects on 8 in × 8 in and 6 in × 6 in tiles (coloured): (a) *Macbeth and the witches.* (b) *Hamlet and Yorick.* (c) *Prince Hotspur — Henry Falstaff.* (d) *Sir Andrew Sir Toby Clown.* (e) *Hotspur Lord Anthony.* (f) *Sampson Balthasar Baram.* (g) *Katherine Petruchio.* (h)

Pericles Thaisa Simonides. (i) *Prince Hal Poins Falstaff.* (j) *Somerset and Plantagenet.* (k) *Parolles.* (l) *Touchstone Rosalind and Celia.* (m) *Audery Touchstone.* (n) *Ajax and Theresites.*

Mediaeval Leisure Occupations *c* 1877. 6 subjects on 6 in × 6 in tiles. Ladies engaged in medieval occupations (cane body printed and painted in brown, coloured): (a) *Writing.* (b) *Embroidery.* (c) *Painting.* (d) *Music.* (e) *Sculpture.* (f) *Astronomy.*

Mediaeval Occupations *c* 1877. (See page 59.) 6 subjects on 6 in × 6 in tiles (cane body printed and painted in brown, coloured): (a) *The blacksmith.* (b) *The artist.* (c) *The gardener.* (d) *The sculptor.* (e) *The alchemist.* (f) *The musician.*

Musicians *c* 1878. 12 subjects on 6 in × 6 in tiles (coloured and blue monochrome) (a) *Cymbals.* (b) *Fiddle* (violin). (c) *Double flute.* (d) *Cello.* (e) *Lute.* (f) *Pan pipes.* (g) *Troubadour fiddle.*

Nursery Rhymes *c* 1880. 12 (?) subjects on 6 in × 6 in tiles contained within a circular frame with ribbon corners. 8 subjects recorded (coloured): (a) *Simple Simon.* (b) *Red Riding Hood.* (c) *King Cole.* (d) *Tom Ye Piper's Son.* (e) *Old Mother Hubbard.* (f) *Little Bo Peep.* (g) *Little Boy Blue.* (h) *Taffy (Was a Welshman).*

Oriental Trades *c* 1880. 17 subjects on 6 in × 6 in tiles depicting orientals at work (coloured figure on a plain background with a simple lined border; coloured figure on a plain background with a blue circular border).

Mediaeval Occupations *c* 1880. 13 subjects on 6 in × 6 in tiles (coloured): (a) *Potter.* (b) *The carpenter.* (c) *The tilt.* (d) *Bowling* (skittles). (e) *Night watchman.* (f) *Digging.* (g) *Armourer.* (h) *Bowman.* (i) *Merchant.* (j) *Crossbowman.* (k) *Maidservant.* (l) *Fisherman.* (m) *Musketeer.*

The Hunt *c* 1878. (See page 57.) 16 subjects on 6 in × 6 in tiles illustrating the events of a wild boar and stag hunt. Full series of 24 (?) probably includes a fox hunt (coloured).

Little Lord Fauntleroy. 4 subjects on 8 in × 8 in tiles (blue monochrome): (a) *The artist.* (b) *The musician.* (c) *The writer.* (d) *The astronomer.*

Frog Series *c* 1880. (See page 59.) 12 subjects on 6 in × 6 in tiles illustrating the exploits of an adventurous frog (blue monochrome).

Minton Hollins Picture Tiles (1870-1900)

Nursery Rhymes (J. Moyr Smith). (See page 55.) 10 subjects printed on 6 in × 6 in and 8 in × 8 in tiles (black on white, brown on white, black on white tinted with pink): (a) *Jack Sprat Could Eat No Fat.* (b) *See-Saw Marjory Daw.* (c) *Little Miss Muffett.* (d) *Old King Cole.* (e) *The Queen of Hearts.* (f) *Little Jack Horner.* (g) *Sing a Song of Sixpence.* (h) *Jack and Jill.* (i) *Little Bo Peep.* (j) *Humpty Dumpty.*

Shakespeare. (See page 54.) 10 subjects printed on 6 in × 6 in tiles (pink on white): (a) *Juliet's death.* (b) *Ferdinand and Miranda.* (c) *Juliet and nurse.* (d) *Othello relating his adventures.* (e) *Hamlet with skull.* (f) *Lorenzo and Jessica.* (g) *Orlando and Rosalind.* (h) *Orlando.* (i) *Bassanio with letter.* (j) *Laertes and Ophelia.*

English History (J. Moyr Smith). (See page 55). 10 subjects printed on 6 in × 6 in tiles (grey monochrome tinted with sepia on white): (a) *Murder of A. Becket: 1171.* (b) *Magna Carta: 1215.* (c) *Hereward at Ely: 1071.* (d) *Richard I.* (e) *Philippa pleading with Edward III: 1347.* (f) *The Armada in Sight: 1588.* (g) *The Gunpowder plot: 1605.* (h) *Sir Philip Sydney at Zutphen: 1586.*

Authors and Their Works. (See page 54.) 10 subjects printed on 8 in × 8 in tiles (brown on beige): (a) *Una and the Satyrs — Spenser.* (b) *The Ancient Mariner — Coleridge.* (c) *Sardanpalus — Byron.* (d) *Aeneas and Dido — Virgil.* (e) *The Jolly Beggars — Burns.* (f) *Patient Griselda — Chaucer.* (g) *Francesca — Dante.* (h) *Walpurgis Night — Goethe.* (i) *The Witch of Atlas — Shelley.* (j) *The Death of Marmion — Scott.*

Aesop's Fables. (See page 54.) 10 subjects printed on 6 in × 6 in and 8 in × 8 in tiles. Circular frame with leaf motif in corners (black on royal blue, navy blue on white, black on cream, green on white with yellow tinted border): (a) *Death and the Woodman.* (b) *Dog and His Shadow.* (c) *Dog and the Bees.* (d) *Frog and the Mouse (Rat).* (e) *Pig and the Wolf.* (f) *The Wolf and the Stork.* (g) *The Frogs Who Wanted a King.* (h) *Two Frogs.* (i) *The Wolf in Sheep's Clothing.*

Religious Series. (See page 54.) 10 subjects printed on 6 in × 6 in tiles; central scene within a circular border (turquoise on black, black on white, brown on white, and black on white with red tinted border).

Animals. (See page 55.) 10 subjects printed on 6 in × 6 in tiles (blue on white): (a) *Cattle.* (b) *Sheep.* (c) *Donkeys.* (d) *Ducks.*

Children's Games. (See page 53.) 6 (?) subjects printed and hand tinted on 6 in × 6 in tiles: (a) *Playing skittles.* (b) *Billiards.* (c) *Queue of boys, each with a bouquet to present to a girl.* (d) *Boy holding a gentleman's cloak clear of the ground watched by three girls.* (e) *Girl handing a boy a tray on which is a glass and an apple.*

Times of Day — Peasant Activities. (See page 55.) 4 subjects printed on 8 in × 8 in tiles (purple and white, brown and buff): (a) *Morning.* (b) *Afternoon.* (c) *Evening.* (d) *Night.*

Seasons. (See page 55.) 4 subjects printed on 6 in × 6 in tiles illustrating seasonal activities (brown on beige, and black on blue): (a) *Spring.* (b) *Summer.* (c) *Autumn.* (d) *Winter.*

Theseus and the Crommyonian Sow (Boar) (J. Moyr Smith). (See page 105.) 6 subjects printed on 6 in × 6 in and 8 in × 8 in tiles. Transfer printed and hand coloured.

Oriental Series. 6 (?) subjects printed on 6 in × 6 in tiles depicting orientals at work (grey monochrome and hand coloured): (a) *Man with spear on horseback.* (b) *Fisherman.* (c) *Man rowing boat.* (d) *Duck hunter.*

Maw & Co. Picture Tiles (1870-1900)

Pattern Nos. 1577-1584: **Bird Tiles.** 9 subjects printed on 6 in × 6 in tiles with different geometric borders (black on white): (a) *Cuckoo.* (b) *Partridge.* (c) *Swallow.* (d) *Wren.* (e) *Moorhen.* (f) *Goldfinch.* (g) *Woodpecker.* (h) *Woodcock.*

Bird Tiles. (See page 62.) 12 subjects printed on 6 in × 6 in tiles (white on black): (a) *Blackbird.* (b) *Cuckoo.* (c) *Dove.* (d) *House swallow.* (e) *Kingfisher.* (f) *Partridge.* (g) *Common snipe.* (h) *Skylark.* (i) *Starling.* (j) *Thrush.* (k) *Wagtail.* (l) *Yellowhammer.*

Pattern Nos. 2132-2140: **Seven Ages of Man.** (See catalogue on page 61.) 7 subjects on 6 in × 6 in tiles (black on light blue, black on yellow, black on white, black on grey, black on green): (a) *The infant.* (b) *The schoolboy.* (c) *The lover.* (d) *The soldier.* (e) *Lean and slipper'd pantaloon.* (f) *The justice.* (g) *Second childishness.*

Pattern Nos. 2141-2149: **Religious Series.** (See page 63.) 12 subjects printed on 8 in × 8 in tiles (brown on grey, brown on yellow, brown on cream, blue on white): (a) *Christ entering Jerusalem.* (b) *The rich man and Lazarus.* (c) *The barren fig tree.* (d) *A miracle healing.* (e) *The lost sheep.* (f) *The wicked*

husbandmen. (g) *The sower.* (h) *The Pharisee and the publican.* (i) *The hidden treasure.* (j) *The lost piece of silver.* (k) *The foolish virgins.* (l) *The prodigal son.*

Pattern Nos. 2158-2169: **Signs of the Zodiac.** (See catalogue on page 61.) 12 subjects printed on 6 in × 6 in tiles (brown on yellow, black on green, black on grey, yellow on brown): (a) *Aquarius.* (b) *Pisces.* (c) *Aries.* (d) *Taurus.* (e) *Gemini.* (f) *Cancer.* (g) *Leo.* (h) *Virgo.* (i) *Libra.* (j) *Scorpio.* (k) *Sagittarius.* (l) *Capricorn.*

Pattern No. 2170: **Sol and Luna** (Walter Crane). (See catalogue on page 61.) 2 emblematic tiles of the sun and moon with 3 supplementary infill tiles, classical style, 8 in × 8 in tiles printed and hand painted.

Pattern No. 2171: **Nursery Rhyme Tiles** (Walter Crane). (See catalogue on page 61.) Vertical panel comprising 3 6 in × 6 in tiles with supplementary border tiles of plant growing from pot. Hand painted. (a) *Tom Tucker.* (b) *Mistress Mary.* (c) *Little Boy Blue.*

Pattern No. 2172: **Little Bo Peep Panel** (Walter Crane). (See catalogue on page 61.) 6 in × 6 in tiles with supplementary classical style tiles printed and hand painted.

Pattern No. 2173: **Little Bo Peep Panel** (Walter Crane). (See catalogue on page 61.) 6 in × 6 in tiles with circular border around a vertical panel of cherubs climbing a daisy. Printed and hand painted.

Pattern No. 2174. **Nursery Rhymes** (Walter Crane). (See catalogue on page 61.) 4 subjects on 6 in × 6 in tiles with supplementary infill classical tiles. Printed and hand coloured. (a) *Jock he was a person.* (b) *Little Brown Betty.* (c) *Tom Tucker.* (d) *Mistress Mary.*

Pattern No. 2175. **Elements** (Walter Crane). (See catalogue on page 61.) 4 subjects on 6 in × 6 in and 8 in × 8 in tiles, with classical-inspired infill tiles. Printed and hand coloured. (a) *Zephyria* (sic). (b) *Terra.* (c) *Ignis.* (d) *Aqua.*

Pattern Nos. 2176-2179: **Seasons and Times of Day** (Walter Crane). (See catalogue on page 61.) 8 subjects on tiles 8 in × 8 in with supplementary infill tiles. Transfer printed and hand painted. (a) *Ver.* (b) *Merides* (sic). (c) *Autumus* (sic). (d) *Aurora.* (e) *Aestas.* (f) *Hiems.* (g) *Vesper.* (h) *Nox.*

Pattern Nos. 2225-2236: **Aesop's Fables** (C. O. Murray). (See page 63.) 12 subjects printed on 6 in × 6 in tiles (brown on white, brown on buff, blue on white): (a) *The Old Man and His Ass.* (b) *Small Fish Better Than None.* (c) *The Goose Which Laid the Golden*

Eggs. (d) *Two Companions and the Bear.* (e) *The Boy Who Cried Wolf.* (f) *The Swan among The Geese.* (g) *Death and the Woodman.* (h) *Milkmaid.* (i) *The Old Man and His Sons.* (j) *Pilgrims and the Oysters.* (k) *Doctors and the Dying Man.* (l) *The Country Man and the Snake.*

Pattern Nos. 2394-2395: **War and Peace.** 2 subjects on 6 in × 12 in tiles symbolic of war and peace.

Pattern Nos. 2410-2421: **Trades.** (See page 63.) 12 subjects printed on 6 in × 6 in tiles (brown on white, black on grey): (a) *Blacksmith.* (b) *Carpenter.* (c) *Forester.* (d) *Tailor.* (e) *Painter.* (f) *Hooper.* (g) *Bricklayer.* (h) *Stonemason.* (i) *Shoemaker.* (j) *Shipwright.* (k) *Navvy.* (l) *Founder.*

Pattern Nos. 2465-2467: **Japanese Series.** (See page 61.) 3 subjects printed on tiles 12 in × 6 in. Geisha Girls (blue on white). 3 subjects printed on tiles 6 in × 6 in. Geisha girls (blue on white).

Pattern Nos. 2517-2519: **Children at Play.** 3 subjects printed on tiles 12 in × 6 in (turquoise on white).

Pattern Nos. 2554-2669. 6 (?) subjects printed on 6 in × 6 in tiles (black on white): (a) *Woman with umbrella.* (b) *Woman climbing steps at the coast.* (c) *Town crier.*

Pattern Nos. 2562-2573: **Husbandry (?).** 12 subjects printed on 6 in × 6 in and 8 in × 8 in tiles (brown on beige): (a) *Woman milking a cow.* (b) *Man cutting wood.* (c) *Digging.* (d) *Shepherdess.*

Pattern Nos. 2575-2580: **Bird Series.** 6 subjects on 6 in × 6 in tiles printed and hand coloured. (2577) *Kingfisher.* (2578) *Grouse.* (2579) *Swallow.* (2580) *Plover.*

Pattern 2592-2597: **Children's Pastimes.** 6 subjects printed on 6 in × 6 in tiles.

Pattern Nos. 2633-2644: **Landscape Scenes.** 12 subjects printed on 12 in × 8 in tiles. 8 of the subjects also printed on 8 in × 8 in tiles (brown on white, blue on white).

Pattern Nos. 2700-2703: **Rivers of Great Britain.** 4 subjects printed on 6 in × 6 in tiles (white on brown): (a) *Shannon.* (b) *Thames.* (c) *Severn.* (d) *Clyde.*

Pattern Nos. 2747-2755: **Muses.** 9 subjects on 6 in × 6 in tiles printed in blue with women in classical dress.

Classical Muses. (See page 62.) 6 (?) subjects printed on 6 in × 6 in tiles with a square centre contained in a wavy line border. (a) *Affection.* (b) *Fortune.* (c) *Industry.* (d) *Practice.*

Carter & Co.
Picture Tile Series (c 1930)

Pattern Nos. BD(CD)1-12: **Blue Dutch & Coloured Dutch** (J. Roulelants). Hand painted on 5 in × 5 in and 6 in × 6 in tiles: (a) *Boy and girl talking on dyke wall.* (b) *Fisherman with net on sea-shore.* (c) *Girl in countryside.* (d) *Girl with basket of eggs.* (e) *Woman in vegetable garden.* (f) *Boy and girl standing watching bonfire.* (g) *Man and woman cutting hay with sickle.* (h) *Windmill in a landscape.* (i) *Boy and girl hoeing field.* (j) *Village scene.* (k) *Church.* (l) *Boats on water-front.*

Pattern Nos. FY1-12: **Farmyard** (E. E. Stickland). (See page 74.) Hand painted on 5 in × 5 in and 6 in × 6 in tiles: (a) *Two geese.* (b) *Windmill.* (c) *Sheep and lamb.* (d) *Cockerel and chickens.* (e) *Hay-ricks.* (f) *Pig and piglet.* (g) *Two ducks.* (h) *Billy-goat.* (i) *Turkey.* (j) *Two rabbits.* (k) *Shire horse.* (l) *Fan-tail doves.*

Pattern Nos. FS1-12: **Fish** (A. Nickols). Hand painted on 5 in × 5 in and 6 in × 6 in tiles depicting swimming deep-sea fish.

Pattern Nos. SF 1-6: **Flowers (SF)** (Truda Carter). Hand painted on 5 in × 5 in and 6 in × 6 in tiles depicting groups of country flowers.

Pattern Nos. SH 1-6: **Flowers (SH)** (Reginald Till). (See page 74.) 6 subjects hand painted on 5 in × 5 in and 6 in × 6 in tiles depicting posies of flowers tied with a ribbon, with corner trefoil motif.

Pattern Nos. SW 1-6: **Flowers (SW)** (Reginald Till). 6 subjects hand painted on 5 in × 5 in tiles depicting figurative flowers.

Pattern Nos. KT1-12: **For the Kitchen** (A. B. Read). 12 subjects hand painted on 5 in × 5 in and 6 in × 6 in tiles: (a) *Baking utensils.* (b) *Pie.* (c) *Fruit.* (d) *Chicken drum-sticks.* (e) *Fresh vegetables.* (f) *Trifle.* (g) *Saucepans.* (h) *Trussed fowl.* (i) *Eggs, flour and mixing bowl.* (j) *Ham.* (k) *Fish in frying-pan.* (l) *Trout on plate.*

Pattern Nos. NR1-6: **Nursery Rhymes** (Dora M. Batty). (See page 75.) 6 subjects hand painted on 5 in × 5 in and 6 in × 6 in tiles. All tiles have a corner trefoil motif: (a) *Mary, Mary, Quite Contrary.* (b) *By Baby Bunting.* (c) *Little Bo Peep.* (d) *Jack and Jill.* (e) *Ride a Cock Horse.* (f) *Little Miss Muffet.*

Pattern Nos. CS1-12: **The Chase** (Edward Bawden). (See page 75.) Hand painted on 5 in × 5 in and 6 in × 6 in tiles: (a) *One large and two small fish.* (b) *An eagle swooping on two birds.* (c) *Two running rabbits and one sitting.* (d) *Two running foxes.* (e) *A partridge below two pheasants, all flying.* (f) *Four running hounds.* (g) *A huntswoman.* (h) *A fisherman.* (i) *A falconer.* (j) *Another huntswoman.* (k) *A huntsman blowing horn.* (l) *Man firing gun.*

Pattern Nos. CC1-9: **The Circus** (Clifford and Rosemary Ellis). Hand painted on 5 in × 5 in and 6 in × 6 in tiles: (a) *High-wire artiste.* (b) *Man balancing ball on stick held in mouth.* (c) *Horse.* (d) *Centre ring with ringmaster and bareback rider* (4 tiles). (e) *Trapeze artiste.* (f) *Seal balancing ball.* (g) *Boxing kangaroo.* (h) *Juggler.* (i) *Zebra.*

Pattern Nos. DG1-6: **Dog Studies** (Cecil Aldin). (See page 74.) 6 tiles depicting comic dogs. Hand painted on 5 in × 5 in and 6 in × 6 in tiles.

Pattern Nos. NT1-7: **Nursery Toys** (Dora M. Batty). 7 subjects designed to complement **Nursery Rhymes**, hand painted on 5 in × 5 in and 6 in × 6 in tiles. All with corner trefoil motif: (a) *Jumping lamb.* (b) *Cockerel.* (c) *Three soldiers.* (d) *Duck and ducklings* (swimming). (e) *Rocking horse.* (f) *Noah's ark.* (g) Supplementary tile with central plant and trefoil borders also intended for use with **Nursery Rhymes**.

Pattern Nos. PB1-12: **Play Box** (A. B. Read). 12 subjects hand painted on 5 in × 5 in and 6 in × 6 in tiles depicting wooden toys: (a) *Chicken and cockerel.* (b) *Fish.* (c) *Owl and birds.* (d) *Male and female gardeners.* (e) *Wedding.* (f) *Drummer and penguins.* (g) *Cart, cyclist and policeman.* (h) *Rocking horse.* (i) *Horse and hound.* (j) *Giraffe.* (k) *Milkmaid and ducks.* (l) *Elephant.*

Pattern Nos. SS(SB)1-6: **Ships** (Reginald Till). 6 subjects hand painted on 5 in × 5 in and 6 in × 6 in tiles in sepia (SS) or blue (SB) monochrome depicting "pseudo Delft" style sailing ships, with barred ox-head corners.

Pattern Nos. SP1-7: **Sporting** (Edward Bawden). 7 subjects contained within a circular border, hand painted on 5 in × 5 in and 6 in × 6 in tiles: (a) *Fox hunting.* (b) *Fishing.* (c) *Punting.* (d) *Shooting.* (e) *Motoring.* (f) *Golfing.* (g) Additional tile with a central sun motif.

Pattern Nos. WB1-7: **Water Birds** (Harold Stabler). 7 subjects hand painted in colour on 5 in × 5 in and 6 in × 6 in tiles: (a) *Guillemot.* (b) *Wagtail.* (c) *Bittern.* (d) *Goose.* (e) *Duck.* (f) *Gull.* (g) Tile with central motif of rushes.

Pattern Nos. DA1-5: **Dairy Subjects** (A. Nickols). 5 panels of 4 tiles, hand painted in colour: (a) *Pond with ducks and geese.* (b) *Two dairy cattle grazing.* (c) *Farm girl with dog.* (d) *Girl milking cow.* (e) *Chicken in front of hay-ricks.*

Craven Dunnill Picture Tiles
(c 1880)

Wild Life. Series of 12 subjects on 6 in × 6 in tiles, transfer printed in brown.

Months of the Year. Series of 12 subjects, transfer printed in brown and polychrome.

Who Killed Cock Robin? (See page 64.) Series of 6 subjects and a complementary tile of the music to the rhyme, transfer printed and hand coloured.

The House That Jack Built. Series of 7 subjects, transfer printed in blue and red.

Malkin Edge & Co.
Picture Tiles (c 1880)

Games Series. 12 subjects printed on 6 in × 6 in tiles (hand coloured and brown on beige): (213) *Croquet.* (215) *Archery.* (216) *Bowls.* (217) *Billiards.* (219) *Cricket.* (220) *Marbles.* (221) *Shuttlecock.* (223) *Leap-frog.* (224) *Ball.* (225) *Chess.* (227) *Skittles.* (228) *Blind man's buff.*

Pattern No. 1190: **Bird Series.** 12 (?) subjects printed on 6 in × 6 in tiles (sepia on ivory).

Pattern No. 1250: **Mothers and Children.** 6 (?) subjects, coloured and plain brown transfer prints within a circular border on 6 in × 6 in tiles. Also on 8 in × 8 in with a square border.

Pattern No. 1316. **Bird Series.** 16 subjects printed on 6 in × 6 in tiles, printed and hand coloured. Also on 8 in × 8 in (No. 1403).

Pattern No. 1343: 4 different Renaissance girls' heads enclosed within a small circle bordered by a larger outer circle.

Pilkingtons

Résumé of the single tiles, panels and series contained in the Glasgow Exhibition catalogue of 1901:

The Senses (Walter Crane). Painted by John Chambers: *Sight, Hearing, Smell, Taste, Touch.* **Anthemion Freize Pattern** (Lewis F. Day); painted in yellow and orange underglaze. **Chinese Pattern** (Lewis F. Day); stencilled in underglaze blue and white. **Fish and Leaf Pattern** (C. F. A. Voysey); impressed tiles coloured with rich blue glaze. **Lemon Tree Design** (C. F. A. Voysey); panel contained 20 different tiles to complete the design, each tile separately impressed. **The Labours** (C. F. A. Voysey); tiles printed in blue underglaze. **Viking Ships** (C. F. A. Voysey); impressed tiles forming a freize of ships. **Feather Leaf Pattern** (Lewis F. Day); embossed tiles in low relief in peacock blue glaze. **Berry Pattern** (Lewis F. Day); embossed tile with the ground deeply incised so as to give a light and dark chequer in the pattern. **Pomegranate Pattern** (Lewis F. Day); panel of incised tiles. **Arab Lattice Panel** (Lewis F. Day); Panel in opus sec tiles contains over 700 separate pieces. **Spring Meadow** (Lewis F. Day). **Peony Pattern** (Lewis F. Day). **Ogee Pattern** (Lewis F. Day). **Panel of Printed Tiles** (L. V. Solon); printed in colour under a coloured glaze. **Sprig Pattern** (Lewis F. Day). **Celtic Pattern** (Lewis F. Day). **Renaissance Pattern** (Lewis F. Day); painted by Miss Briggs. **Clifton Pattern** (Lewis F. Day); painted by Miss A. Tyldersley. **Strap Pattern** (Lewis F. Day); painted by Miss A. Tyldersley. **Nevers Pattern** (Lewis F. Day); painted by Miss A. Tyldersley. **Beech Pattern** (Lewis F. Day); embossed tile design. **Assyrian Pattern** (John Chambers). **Love in the Mist Pattern** (Lewis F. Day). **Iris Pattern** (Lewis F. Day). **Tudor Pattern** (Lewis F. Day). **Apple Blossom** (Lewis F. Day). **Persian Pattern** (Lewis F. Day). **Moresque Pattern** (John Chambers). **Rosette Pattern** (Lewis F. Day). **Japanese Birds** (Lewis F. Day). **Queen of the Tourney** (J. Cooper). **Knights and Heralds** (J Cooper); tiles in low relief. **Welcome** (Florence Steel). **Bell Flower** (Lewis F. Day). **The Rose and the Sweet Pea** (Florence Steel). **Pierced Pattern** (Lewis F. Day); printed in black under brown glaze. **Green Ivy Pattern** (Lewis F. Day); printed in black under crimson glaze. **Coalbrookdale Pattern** (Lewis F. Day). **Rosace Pattern** (Lewis F. Day); printed in colours under brown. **Bird and Lemon Tree** (C. F. A. Voysey); impressed tiles coloured with rich blue glaze. **Vine and Bird** (C. F. A. Voysey); impressed tiles coloured with peacock blue glaze. **The Carnation, The Lily, The Iris, The Rose** (Alphonse Mucha). 3 ft 6 in × 1 ft 6 in (97 cm × 46 cm) panels painted on 6 in × 6 in tiles by John Chambers, Miss Tyldersley and Miss Briggs. **Flora's Train** (Walter Crane). 6 tiles depicting the poppy, cornflower, anemone, daffodil, columbine and bluebell. Modelled by A. J. Kwiatkowski and painted by John Chambers, Miss Tyldersley and Miss Briggs.

Known Examples of George Cartlidge's Work

For Sherwin & Cotton (1882-1911): (a) *Queen Victoria* (1897). (b) *William Ewart Gladstone* (1898). (c) *General Booth* (1904). (d) *Abraham Lincoln* (1909). (e) *Pope Pius X.* (f) *James Sherwin.* (g) *Fred Hodge.* (h) *Tuari Netana.* (i) *Matene Te Nga.* (j) *Bella.* (k) *Sophia.* (l) *Uncle Joe.*

For Adams & Cartlidge (1911-16?) (a) *Austen Chamberlain.*

For J. H. Barratt & Co. (1916-19) (a) *W. M. Hughes.* (b) *Herbert Henry Asquith.* (c) *David Lloyd George.* (d) *T. R. Roosevelt.* (e) *Woodrow Wilson.* (f) *Field Marshall Sir Douglas Haig.* (g) *Admiral Sir John Jellicoe.* (h) *Admiral John J. Pershing.* (i) *Admiral Sir David Beatty.* (j) *General Foch.* (k) *General Smuts.*

In America (1919-20?) (a) *General Warren Harding* (for the Fine Art Ceramic Co.). (b) *General Wood.*

For Barratts (1920?-7) (a) *Conrad Dressler.* (b) *H. C. Sawyer.* (c) *J. H. Boycott.* (d) *E. R. Corn.* (e) *Sydney H. Dodd (1927).* (f) *Thomas Hardy (1924).* (g) *Sydney R. Maw (1924).*

Illustrations of George Cartlidge's work appear on pages 114 and 115.

153

APPENDIX C

British Tile Companies

The following list is of the principal tile manufacturers and decorators in Britain from about 1840. It has been compiled from standard works of reference, a study of local directories, "word of mouth" and information gathered during several years' research. Of necessity, individuals who registered designs or who set up small enterprises have been omitted since these run into hundreds and it would not be practical to include them all. An asterisk indicates that the company used an easily recognizable tile back or trade mark on their wares and these are listed on pages 129-45.

Adams and Bromley: Victoria Works, Hanley, Staffordshire; c 1895. Tile decorators. Probably a continuation of Adams & Bromley — potters (1873-86).

Adams and Cartlidge*: Vine Street, Hanley, Staffordshire; c 1911-16. Wall Tiles.

Architectural Pottery Co.*: Poole, Dorset; 1854-95. Encaustic and plain floor tiles.

Art Tile Co.: Dudley, Worcestershire; c 1896-c 1900. Encaustic and other tiles.

Art Tileries: Stourbridge, Worcestershire; c 1895. Tile decorators.

Atlas Tile Works: Vine Street, Hanley, Staffordshire; 1907-20. Wall tiles.

J. H. Barratt & Co.*: Boothen Tile Works, Stoke, Staffordshire; c 1895-1927. Printed and majolica tiles. Produced some of Cartlidge's portrait tiles.

Barry & Co.: Woodville Tile Works, Burton-on-Trent, Staffordshire; c 1880-c 1890. Encaustic tiles and mosaics.

Bates, Dewsbury & Co.: Mayer Street, Hanley, Staffordshire; c 1896-c 1900. Encaustic tiles.

Birch Tile Co. Ltd.: Clarence Street, Fenton, Staffordshire; c 1896-1900. Encaustic tiles.

J. M. Blashfield: Blackfriars and Millwall, London; 1836-58. At Stamford (Lincs.) 1858-75. Encaustic and other tiles. Architectural terracottas from 1851. An early user of Copeland and Garrett's plain (red and black) floor tiles (1836). In 1839 laid a mosaic floor at Deepdene. "Designs for Mosaic Pavements" by Owen Jones produced for the firm in 1842. Own tiles made from c 1840 after association with Herbert Minton.

T. & R. Boote*: Waterloo Pottery, Burslem, Staffordshire; 1842-1962. Tiles from 1850.

T. G. & F. Booth*: Church Bank Pottery, Tunstall, Staffordshire; 1883-91. Earthenware and tiles.

Broseley Tileries: Broseley, Shropshire; c 1860-1910. Roofing tiles, some plain and coloured floor tiles.

Robert Brown & Co.: Paisley Earthenware Works, Scotland; 1876-1933. Earthenware and tiles.

Brown Westhead Moore & Co.: Cauldon Place, Hanley, Staffordshire; 1862-1904. Earthenware, some tiles marked "Ravenscroft Patent".

Burmantofts Pottery*: Leeds, Yorkshire; 1858-1914. Bricks and pipes until 1880 when Wilcox & Co. began manufacture of art pottery, tiles and architectural faience. After 1904 became Leeds Fireclay Co. Ltd. architectural faience and terracotta.

T. W. Camm: Brewery Street, later High Street, Smethwick, Staffordshire; 1866-c 1870. Camm Bros. from 1870-80. Tile decorators only (hand painted). Tiles marked with firm's name.

Campbell Brick & Tile Co.*: Stoke, Staffordshire; 1875-82. Campbell Tile Co. from 1882. Wall and floor tiles.

Carlisle Brick & Tile Works: Carlisle, Cumberland; c 1885-1900. Plain floor and decorated wall tiles.

Carter & Co.*: Poole, Dorset; 1873-1964. Architectural faience, encaustic and other floor tiles, hand-painted, printed and majolica tiles. Carter, Stabler & Adams set up 1921 producing earthenware. Became Poole Pottery 1963.

Carter Johnson & Co. St. George's Tile Works, Worcester; c 1870-95. Encaustic tiles.

Chamberlain & Co.*: Warmstrey House, Worcester; 1840-8. After merger of Fight & Barr with Chamberlains, Barr continued to make encaustic tiles at the old premises, joined briefly by Fleming St. John. Bought share in Wright's patent 1844.

Cleveland Tile Co.: Liverpool Road, Stoke, Staffordshire; 1900-5. Printed tiles.

Copeland & Garrett*: Spode Works, Stoke, Staffordshire. Earthenware and porcelain. Some plain floor tiles from c 1834, encaustic tiles from c 1837-40, wall tiles from 1840-1903. Became W. T. Copeland in 1847 (& Sons, 1867).

W. & E. Corn*: Navigation Road, Burslem, Staffordshire; 1864-91. Earthenware. Top Bridge Works, Longport; 1891-1904. Additional premises at Albert Street, Tunstall, Staffordshire. Printed and majolica wall tiles. Name changed to Corn Bros. c 1894.

Craven Dunnill & Co.*: Jackfield, Nr. Ironbridge, Shropshire; 1871-1951. Formerly Hargreaves & Craven. Wall and floor tiles.

Crystal Porcelain Co.: Cobridge, Nr. Stoke, Staffordshire; c 1875-81 Industrial porcelain and tiles.

Crystal Porcelain Pottery Co.*: Cobridge, Nr. Stoke, Staffordshire; 1881-90. Took over the above company. Continued with industrial porcelain and tiles, introduced majolica tiles. 1890 changed name to Crystal Porcelain Tile Co., manufacturing encaustic, majolica and porcelain tiles. Continued until c 1897.

Decorative Art Tile Pottery Co.*: Bryan Street, Hanley, Staffordshire; 1885-1902. Thought to be decorators only. Some embossed tiles are known probably made for the company elsewhere.

Della Robbia Co. Ltd.*: Birkenhead, Cheshire; 1894-1906. Started by Harold Rathbone (pupil of Madox Brown), and Conrad Dressler emulating work of Luca Della Robbia. Hand-made plaques rather than tiles.

W. De Morgan*: Chelsea, London; 1872-82. Merton Abbey, Surrey; 1882-8. Fulham, London; 1888-1907. Unique hand-painted tiles.

Walter Pen Dennis: Ruabon, Wales; c 1891-1901. Tiles.

Doulton & Co. Ltd.*: Lambeth, London; 1858-c 1915. Architectural faience, floor and wall tiles, hand-painted panels. Lambeth Studio; 1860. Hand-decorated tiles and panels, many signed. Some tiles decorated at Burslem Studio from 1882.

William Eardley: Lichfield Street, Hanley, Staffordshire; c 1887. (Encaustic?) tiles.

J. C. Edwards*: Ruabon, Wales; c 1870-1958. Architectural faience and terracottas, **encaustic and other floor tiles.** Majolica, printed and lustre tiles.

William England & Sons: Bloomsbury, London; c 1870-c 1900. Encaustic tiles and mosaics, some decorated wall tiles.

Samuel Fielding & Co.*: Railway Pottery from 1879, Devon Pottery from 1911. Stoke earthenwares, printed and majolica tiles. Trade name "Crown Devon" introduced in 1913.

T. Forrester & Sons: Thought to be decorators only, c 1895.

Gateshead Art Pottery: East Street, Gateshead, Durham; 1884-c 1900. Hand-decorated tiles and earthenware.

Gibbons Hinton & Co.*: Brierley Hill, Staffordshire; 1883-c 1950. Printed and majolica wall tiles.

Gibbs & Canning: Glasscote, Nr. Tamworth, Staffordshire; 1847-c 1904. Architectural terracottas, sanitary wares. Della Robbia type plaques, etc.

William Godwin (& Son)*: Lugwardine, Hereford; 1851-63. At Withington from 1863-1927. Encaustic and other decorative tiles.

Henry Godwin (& Hewitt)*: Victoria Tile Works, Hereford; 1878. Godwin & Hewitt 1882-1909. Godwin & Thynne 1909-25. Wide range of encaustic and decorative tiles. Later architectural faience and slabbed fireplaces.

Joseph Hamblett: Piercy Brick & Tile Works, West Bromwich, Staffordshire; c 1873-c 1890. Terracottas and sanitary ware, some plain floor tiles.

Hawes & Co.: Holborn, London; c 1876-c 1880. Printed and plain floor tiles.

Hopkins & Co.: Tunstall, Staffordshire; c 1896. Enamelled tile manufacturers.

Jackson Bros.: Castlefield, Hanley, Staffordshire; c 1887.

Jeffrey Tiles Ltd.: Hereford; 1927-58. Slabbed fireplaces and glazed wall tiles.

H. & R. Johnson*: Crystal Tile Works, Cobridge, Staffordshire; 1901. Highgate Tile Works, Tunstall, Staffordshire; 1916. Printed and majolica tiles. Amalgamated with Richards Tiles (1968) and now incorporates many of the 20th-century survivors of the tile industry: Campbell Tile Co., Minton Hollins & Co., T. & R. Boote, Malkin Tiles, Sherwin & Cotton, Maw & Co.

Lea & Boulton*: High Street, Tunstall, Staffordshire; c 1896-1902. Wide range of encaustic and other tiles.

Leeds Art Pottery & Tile Co.: Leeds, Yorkshire; c 1890-1901. Earthenwares, art pottery, architectural faience and tiles.

Lloyds Tiles: Enakel Tileworks, Hereford; c 1925. Slabbed fireplaces.

London Decorating Co.: London; c 1880. Encaustic tiles. Walter Crane was art superintendent.

Malkin Edge & Co.*: Newport Works, Burslem, Staffordshire; 1866. Encaustic, printed and majolica tiles. Became Malkin Tiles c 1900.

Mansfield Brothers: Woodville Art Pottery Works, Woodville & Church Gresley, Burton-on-Trent, Staffordshire; c 1890-1957. Earthenwares and encaustic tiles.

Marsden Tile Co.*: Dale Street, Burslem, Staffordshire; c 1880-1918. Printed and majolica wall tiles. Sole producer of a patent interlocking tile which was absolutely secure when fixed. Also patented rainbow-effect glazing technique.

Maw & Co.*: Worcester; 1850-52. Benthall Works, Broseley, Shropshire; 1852-83. Then at Jackfield, Shropshire until 1969. Tiles of every description, some art pottery.

Alfred Meakin Ltd.*: Victoria Pottery, Tunstall, Staffordshire; 1875. Earthenwares, transfer-printed tiles until c 1910.

Mintons*: Confused history of trade names, dates and personalities. (See page 47.)

Henry Abraham Ollivant*: Etruscan Tile Works, Cliff Vale, Stoke, Staffordshire; c 1890-1908. Transfer-printed and majolica tiles.

Peakes: c 1890. Terracottas and plain floor tiles.

Photo Decorated Tile Co.*: Tutbury, Nr. Derby; 1897-8. Photographically decorated tiles.

Pilkingtons Tile & Pottery Co. Ltd.*: Clifton Junction, Manchester; 1892. Encaustic and other floor tiles, printed, majolica and hand-decorated tiles and panels.

Rhodes Tile Co.*: Reginald Street Works, Tunstall, Staffordshire; 1902-c 1906. Art Nouveau majolica wall tiles.

Henry Richards Tile Co.*: Pinnox Works, Tunstall, Staffordshire; 1902-31. Majolica and plain wall tiles. Later merged with Campbell Tile Co. and H. & R. Johnson.

Sherwin & Cotton*: Vine Street, Hanley, Staffordshire; 1877-1911. Transfer-printed and majolica wall tiles. Well known for barbotine work. Produced Cartlidge's portrait tiles.

Shrigley & Hunt*: London and Lancaster. Decorators only. Used Copeland tiles.

T. A. Simpson & Co. Ltd.*: Furlong Tile Works, Burslem, Staffordshire; c 1885-1969. Printed and majolica tiles.

W. B. Simpson & Sons*: St. Martin's Lane and The Strand, London; c 1870-c 1910. Decorators. Had tiles made for them by Maw & Co. Also designed mosaics.

George Skey & Co.: Wilnecote Works,

Tamworth, Staffordshire; c 1860-1900. Architectural terracottas and plain floor tiles.

E. Smith & Co.*: Coalville, Leicestershire; c 1885-c 1900. Transfer-printed tiles. Also trading as the Midland Brick & Terra Cotta Co.; 1859-1900. Terracottas and sanitary wares.

Smith, Ford & Jones: Cleveland Pottery, Burslem, Staffordshire; c 1885-95. Then Smith & Ford at Lincoln Pottery, Burslem; 1895-8. Earthenware and tiles.

W. T. H. Smith Ltd.: Cable Pottery, Longport, Staffordshire; 1898-1905. Earthenwares and tiles.

Staffordshire Tileries*: Probably J. & M. P. Bell, Stafford Street, Glasgow; 1842-1928. Earthenwares and china, some printed tiles.

Steele & Wood*: London Road, Stoke, Staffordshire; 1874-c 1895. Earthenwares and tiles.

Stone & Co.: Nonesuch Pottery, Ewell & Epsom, Surrey; 1866-c 1898. Terracottas and plain floor tiles.

Stubbs & Hodgart*: Portland Tile Works, Burslem, Staffordshire; 1890-c 1900. Majolica Art Nouveau tiles.

C. P. Sutcliffe & Sons*: Higher Broughton, Manchester; 1885-1901. Transfer-printed and majolica tiles.

George Swift Ltd.: Binns Road, Liverpool; c 1900. Wall and floor tiles.

Robert Minton Taylor*: See Minton.

H. & G. Thynne: Hereford; 1925-57. Slabbed fireplaces, architectural faience, some moulded tiles.

J. & W. Wade*: Flaxman Tile Works, Burslem, Staffordshire; c 1884-1904. Modelled majolica and transfer-printed tiles.

T. W. Walkers Patent Encaustic & Mosaic Ornamental Brick & Tile Manufactory*: East Quay Road, Poole, Dorset; 1860-73. Encaustic tiles and mosaics.

Warick Savage & Co.: Burslem, Staffordshire; c 1900. Embossed tiles, earthenwares, ceramic transfers and general printing.

Webbs Worcester Tileries*: Rainbow Hill, Worcester; 1870-1900. Encaustic and transfer-printed tiles.

Josiah Wedgwood & Sons*: Etruria, Staffordshire. Tile production from c 1780. Dust-pressed tiles from 1867. Encaustic, transfer-printed and majolica tiles until c 1900. Some individual tiles made or printed on T. & R. Boote's tiles, until 1929.

Wood & Co.: Boothen Road Works, Stoke, Staffordshire; c 1885. Encaustic tiles.

George Wooliscroft & Sons*: Chesterton, Etruria and Hanley, Staffordshire; 1849. Encaustic and plain floor tiles, wide range of decorative wall tiles.

Glossary

Barbotine: A process whereby the design is painted onto the tile in coloured slips.

Biscuit: The unglazed, fired body of the tile; so called because after the initial high-temperature firing the tile looks like a dry biscuit.

Blunging: The action of mixing clay with water by the use of slow moving paddles in a container called a blunger.

Bottle Oven: The kiln used for the biscuit firing; so called because its shape resembles a large bottle.

Collodion: A solution of cellulose nitrate in a mixture of alcohol and ether, used by early photographers in the making of a photographic emulsion.

Dado: The lower half of a wall above the skirting.

Delft (Delftware): A generic term for all kinds of opaque, white tin-glazed earthenware including tiles. Delft is a town in Holland which manufactured these sorts of wares.

Die: The metal or plaster-of-Paris plates that were used to shape the tile in the dust press.

Dust Clay: Finely ground, sieved and dried clay used for the manufacture of tiles by dust pressing.

Dust Pressing: The action of forming a tile from dust clay in a press which compacted the clay between two dies. Patented by Richard Prosser in 1840.

Earthenware: A generic term for pottery, more commonly used to describe pottery with a coarse texture.

Émaux Ombrants: Technique of "ponding" glaze on relief tiles to achieve gradation of tone.

Emulsion: A coating containing light-sensitive salts.

Enamels: Colours applied over glaze and fired at a relatively low temperature.

Encaustic: A tile with an inlaid pattern, usually used on the floor and made from either plastic- or dust clay.

Embossed: Tile with a relief pattern moulded on the surface.

Faience: Strictly speaking: tin-glazed earthenware, but more usually applied to all kinds of architectural ceramics, structural as well as decorative. Word derives from the Italian town Faenza.

Glaze: The impervious glass-like coating on the surface of a tile. Applied after the biscuit firing and any subsequent decoration, and fired in a Glost kiln.

Glost Kiln: Small kiln used for glazing.

Hardening On: A low-temperature firing to fix underglaze colours and transfers.

Half Tone: The reduction of a photograph (or drawing) to a series of dots for continuous tone reproduction.

Incised Decoration: Scribed into the surface of a plastic-clay tile.

Intaglio: An indented pattern, the opposite of relief.

Lustre: A metallic, reflective surface on the glaze of a tile.

Majolica: Originally applied to tin-glazed wares. Term used after 1850 to describe a transparent or opaque coloured glaze applied to embossed tiles.

Pâte sur Pâte: a form of decoration in which a relief pattern is built up by repeated applications of thin white slip.

Plastic Clay: The normal "wet" clay used in the manufacture of pottery, porcelain and tiles — can be moulded and shaped by hand. All tiles were made of plastic clay prior to the introduction of dust pressing.

Pouncing: The action of dusting charcoal through a pricked stencil to form the outline of the design on the tile, ready for subsequent painting.

Press: Machine for making tiles from dust clay, hand operated at first, later driven by steam.

Prosser's Patent: See Dust Pressing.

Quarry Tiles: Plain, one-colour floor tiles, usually black or red.

Refractory: Resistant to the melting effects of heat.

Saggar: A refractory box in which the tiles were fired to protect them from the direct heat of the kiln.

Sgraffito: A decorative technique in which the tile was coated with slip and the design scratched through to reveal the clay underneath.

Slip: A liquid clay used to coat a tile prior to decoration; and in a thicker consistency, to inlay plastic-clay encaustic tiles. Also used for the lines in tube lining.

Terracotta: Literally: red earth. Used for architectural decoration and faience. At first limited to reds and browns, but later could be coloured and glazed.

Tesserae: Components of a tesselated pavement, comprised of individual plain-coloured tiles laid to form a geometric pattern.

Tile: An individual flat clay slab, usually not more than 12 in × 6 in. Larger single units and porcelain slabs are usually referred to as plaques. A group of tiles making up a design or picture are generally referred to as panels.

Transfer Printing: The most commonly applied method of decoration. A print was taken from a master plate and later applied to the tile surface.

Tube Lining: A decorative technique in which raised seams of clay are applied which separate areas of coloured glazes.

Vitrification: The process whereby a material is subjected to heat until it fuses into a glass-like substance. If a tile was subjected to prolonged firing, the body became highly vitrified and was thus non-porous.

Bibliography

Anscombe, I. & Gere. C., *Arts and Crafts in Britain and America*, Academy (1978).

Aslin, Elizabeth, *The Aesthetic Movement*, Paul Elek (1969).

Barnard, Julian, *The Decorative Tradition*, Architectural Press (1973).

Barnard, Julian, *Victorian Ceramic Tiles*, Studio Vista (1972).

Berendsen, Ann, *A General History of Tiles*, Faber (1967).

Blake, William P., *Ceramic Art: A Report on Pottery, Porcelain, Tiles, Terra Cotta and Bricks*, London (1875).

Bourry, E., *A Treatise on Ceramic Industries*, Scott Greenwood (1911).

Chaffers, *Marks and Monograms on Pottery and Porcelain*, Reeves & Turner, 14th edition (1932).

Crane, Walter, *The Baby's Opera* (1877), republished by Pan Books (1974).

Crane, Walter, *The Baby's Bouquet* (1877), republished by Pan Books (1974).

Crane, Walter, *The Baby's Own Alphabet*, Routledge (1873).

Crane, Walter, *An Artist's Reminiscences*, Methuen (1907).

Coysh, A. W., *British Art Pottery*, David & Charles (1976).

Cushion, J. P., *Pocket Book of British Ceramic Marks*, Faber (1959).

Day, Lewis F., *Everyday Art*, Batsford (1882).

Dennis, Richard, *Doulton Stoneware Pottery (1870-1925)*, London (1971).

Dennis, Richard, *Doulton Pottery from the Lambeth and Burslem Studios (1873-1939)*, London (1975).

Dixon, R., and Muthesius, Stefan, *Victorian Architecture*, Thames & Hudson (1978).

Dresser, Christopher, *Principles of Decorative Design*, reprinted St. Martins Academy (1973).

Engen, Rodney, K., *Kate Greenaway*, Academy (1976).

Engen, Rodney, K., *Walter Crane as a Book Illustrator*, Academy (1975).

Eyles, Desmond, *Royal Doulton (1815-1965)*, Hutchinson (1965).

Furnival, W. J., *Leadless Decorative Tiles, Faience and Mosaic*, W. J Furnival (1904).

Gaunt, W. and Clayton-Stamm, M. D. E., *William De Morgan*, Studio Vista (1971).

Glass, Frederick J., *Drawing Design and Craftwork*, Batsford (1920).

Godden, Geoffrey A., *Antique Glass and China Under £5*, Barker (1966).

Godden, Geoffrey A., *Encyclopaedia of British Pottery and Porcelain Marks*, Barrie & Jenkins (1964).

Hamilton, David, *Architectural Ceramics*, Thames & Hudson (1978).

Henry, W. Ethelbert and Ward, H. Snowden, *Photo Ceramics*, Dawbarn & Ward (c 1895).

Jewitt, Llewellynn, *The Ceramic Art of Great Britain*, 2 volumes, Virtue & Co, Volume I (1878); Volume II, 2nd edition (1883).

Klamkin, Marian, *The Collector's Book of Wedgwood*, David & Charles (1971).

Lane, Arthur, *A Guide to the Collection of Tiles at the Victoria and Albert Museum*, H.M.S.O., 2nd edition (1960).

Leighton, John, *Suggestions in Design*, Paddington Press, reprinted (1977).

Lemmon, Hans Van, *Tiles, A Collector's Guide*, Souvenir Press (1979).

Lockett, Terence A., *Collecting Victorian Tiles*, Antique Collectors Club (1979).

Lomax, Abraham, *Royal Lancastrian Pottery (1900-1938)*, Lomax (1959).

McCarthy, James F., *Great Industries of Great Britain Vol. III*, Cassell (1878-80).

Ray, Anthony, *English Delftware Tiles*, Faber (1974).

Rhead, G. W. & F. A., *Staffordshire Pots and Potters*, Hutchinson & Co. (1906).

Rose, Andrea, *Pre-Raphaelites*, Phaidon (1977).

Thomas, E. Lloyd, *Victorian Art Pottery*, Guildart (1974).

Schmutzler, Robert, *Art Nouveau*, Thames & Hudson (1977).

Smith, J. Moyr, *Album of Decorative Figures*, Sampson Low (1882).

Smith, J. Moyr, *Ornamental Interiors Ancient and Modern*, London (1887).

Wright, J., *Mediaeval Floor Tiles*, Baker (1975).

Museum Publications

Allwood, Rosamond, *Victorian Tiles*, catalogue of an exhibition at Wolverhampton Art Gallery 1978.

Arts Council of Great Britain, *From Today Painting is Dead: The Beginnings of Photography*, catalogue, Victoria and Albert Museum (16 March-14 May 1972).

Atterbury, Paul and Irvine Louise, *The Doulton Story*, catalogue, Victoria and Albert Museum (1979).

Atterbury, Paul and Aslin, Elizabeth, *Minton (1798-1910)*, catalogue, Victoria and Albert Museum 1976.

Eames, E. S., *A Handbook of Mediaeval Tiles*, British Museum (1968).

Hawkins, Jennifer, *Poole Potteries*, Victoria and Albert Museum (1978).

Herbert, Tony, *The Jackfield Decorative Tile Industry*, Ironbridge Gorge Museum Trust (1978).

Pinkham, Roger, *Catalogue of Pottery by William De Morgan*, Victoria and Albert Museum (1973).

Other Sources

Atterbury, Paul and Lockett, Terry, "The Work of William Wise", *Antique Dealers and Collectors Guide* (July 1978).

Building News (1867-1904).

Burrows Hereford (1898).

Carter & Co. Pattern Books.

Copeland Pattern Books.

Doulton, *Pictures in Pottery* (1904).

Eastlake, Charles, *Hints on Household Tastes*.

Franco-British Exhibition Illustrated Review (1908).

Hereford Journal.

Hereford Times.

Illustrated London News (21 October 1868).

Kellys Trade Directories

Knowles, Eric, "Photographic Portrait Tiles", *Antique Collector* (August 1977).

Little Burgh Directory and Gazette (1876-7).

Minton Archives.

Account of the Manufacture of Pilkington Tiles and Making of Royal Lancastrian Pottery (1933).

Photographic Journal (1860 and 1896).

Pottery Gazette (1878-1905).

Pottery and Glass Trades Journal (1877).

Richards Tiles' Story of Richards (1951).

Sotheby's Belgravia Catalogues (1971-9).

Staffordshire Sentinel (11 March 1905).

Wedgwood Archives, Keele University.

Index

Page numbers in *italic* refer to the illustrations